Praise for *Intentional Tarot*

"This tarot book is a refreshing change in so many ways … Hesselroth's revolutionary method of Intentional Tarot is amazingly potent … The bulk of the book is a strong outline of suggestions in using each card within the four-part Intentional spread: My Understanding, My Goal, My Promise, and My Gratitude. Also, the organic approach to the classic Fool's Journey is simply awe inspiring."

—Nancy Antenucci, author of *Psychic Tarot*

T0275399

INTENTIONAL
TAROT

©Maggie Anderson

About the Author

Denise Hesselroth (Minneapolis) has been a student of tarot for more than forty years. Since retiring from the state department of transportation (MN-DOT), where she was a "data geek" who kept inventory of roadway miles, she has had more time to devote to her tarot studies and other interests. Costume shop manager at a local theater, she also enjoys playing mahjong with her neighbors. She is thrilled to finally be playing in several RPG (role playing games) groups and is a dedicated "Critter" who looks forward to watching Critical Role every Thursday. Denise is a widow with two grown daughters of whom she is immensely proud. She is a semi-active member of the Minnesota tarot community and has presented at the annual North Star Tarot Conference. She posts Intentional Tarot spreads at intentionaltarotbook.com.

DENISE HESSELROTH

INTENTIONAL TAROT

USING THE CARDS WITH PURPOSE

LLEWELLYN PUBLICATIONS
WOODBURY, MINNESOTA

Intentional Tarot: Using the Cards with Purpose © 2020 by Denise Hesselroth. All rights reserved. No part of this book may be used or reproduced in any manner whatsoever, including internet usage, without written permission from Llewellyn Publications, except in the case of brief quotations embodied in critical articles and reviews.

FIRST EDITION
Second Printing, 2021

Book design by Samantha Penn
Cover design by Shannon McKuhen
Editing by Laura Kurtz
Interior art by Llewellyn Classic Tarot

Llewellyn Publications is a registered trademark of Llewellyn Worldwide Ltd.

Library of Congress Cataloging-in-Publication Data
Names: Hesselroth, Denise, author.
Title: Intentional tarot : using the cards with purpose / Denise Hesselroth.
Description: First edition. | Woodbury, Minnesota : Llewellyn Publications,
    2020. | Summary: "Tarot card meanings as well as spreads. Includes
    keyword list"—Provided by publisher.
Identifiers: LCCN 2019040317 (print) | LCCN 2019040318 (ebook) | ISBN
    9780738762579 (paperback) | ISBN 9780738762609 (ebook)
Subjects: LCSH: Tarot.
Classification: LCC BF1879.T2 H47 2020 (print) | LCC BF1879.T2 (ebook) |
    DDC 133.3/2424—dc23
LC record available at https://lccn.loc.gov/2019040317
LC ebook record available at https://lccn.loc.gov/2019040318

Llewellyn Worldwide Ltd. does not participate in, endorse, or have any authority or responsibility concerning private business transactions between our authors and the public.

All mail addressed to the author is forwarded but the publisher cannot, unless specifically instructed by the author, give out an address or phone number.

Any internet references contained in this work are current at publication time, but the publisher cannot guarantee that a specific location will continue to be maintained. Please refer to the publisher's website for links to authors' websites and other sources.

Llewellyn Publications
A Division of Llewellyn Worldwide Ltd.
2143 Wooddale Drive
Woodbury, MN 55125-2989
www.llewellyn.com

Printed in the United States of America

To my daughters, Emily and Maggie,
with love.

Contents

Acknowledgments

At the Twin Cities Tarot Collective's 2018 North Star Tarot Conference, my name was drawn as the lucky recipient of a series of Reason for Being sessions with James Wells. The idea that I should write a book about my ideas for praying with tarot came to me as a result of these sessions.

Many thanks to James and the conference coordinators Nancy Antenucci, Melanie Weber, and Michael Foster. Special thanks to Nancy for her helpful feedback, and my anonymous friend for proofreading the manuscript. At Llewellyn I would like to thank Barbara Moore for developing this book, Laura Kurtz for editing, Samantha Penn for the interior design, and Shannon McKuhen for the beautiful cover art.

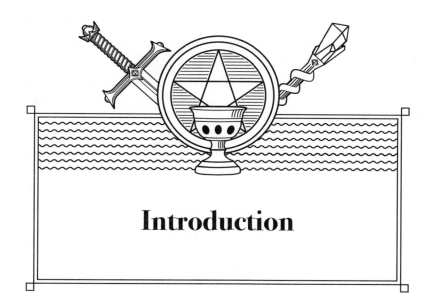

Introduction

The tarot has been a part of my life for more than forty years, yet it's only recently that I feel I've graduated from perpetual beginner to novice. Through those years I've realized that it's perfectly okay to hardly ever read for others; to have never been paid for the few times I brought the cards out to read for friends and family; to own many decks and enjoy finding the next and the next, even if I always read from the same one; and to still open up a book to help me remember the core theme of a card. Working with the cards has kept me connected with the mystery and magic of the world that can be easily overlooked as I go about my average daily life.

One rarely discussed way of working with the tarot cards is a method I've taken to calling Intentional Tarot. In this method of using the tarot cards, we are literally doing the opposite of a traditional tarot reading—we start with an answer instead of a question. We select the cards face up instead of face down. We send our intentions out instead of pulling interpretations in. We attempt to change the world instead of hoping to change our lives. We become active participants instead of passive recipients.

As a complete nobody in the tarot world, I can't pretend to have deeper insights into how to read the cards than the current masters in the field, those who have made their entire lives a full devotion to studying, practicing, and teaching the tarot. I come to the table as someone who has always been interested in the tarot, who looks through the companion book of a new deck a few times each year, and who still struggles with remembering all the cards and what they mean even after forty years. With this book, I hope to offer the tarot community two things:

1. For the perpetual beginner, I have some ideas and methods that have helped me to finally get "off book" and do readings for my friends and family without looking to my books and notes for help. However, the book I refer to in that phrase does not refer to *this* book. I am under no delusion that I could write a book that would bring someone to a deep understanding of the meanings of the tarot cards. The books that I hope to help you put aside will be the ones you already own, be they classics in the field, or companion books to your favorite decks, or online resources you can check with your phone, or any other materials you've collected to help teach yourself how to read the tarot.

2. For anyone interested in tarot, I'm offering a detailed look at what I'm calling the Intentional Tarot method for using the cards. This method involves the rarely discussed idea of using the tarot cards in a non-random manner. In Intentional Tarot, we consciously select specific cards for a specific goal and send our intentions for that goal out to the universe. In the reverse from the traditional process, we begin with an outcome that we desire and select cards that indicate that outcome. Like most tarot books, a large portion of this work is dedicated to information about each of the seventy-eight cards. However, you will find the majority of that section, chapter 4, is focused on examples of card *intentions* to give you ideas for how to practice Intentional Tarot; there is less focus on card *interpretations* to be used in traditional tarot readings.

There are many excellent books of card interpretations available, ranging from the beginner level to deep psychological Jungian essays, from classic phrases to quirky insights specific to only one deck. I have kept to the very basic meanings of the cards and encourage you to find richer interpretations for your traditional tarot study in any of the many tarot resources available. Above all, your greatest resource will be your own practice and experience.

Traditional tarot is both intimate and inward-facing. By interpreting the cards, we hope to gain personal insights and reach a deeper understanding of ourselves and our situations. Intentional Tarot is simultaneously intimate and outward-facing. We articulate our most personal intentions and send them out in hopes of fulfillment. The main purpose of this book is to show how we can use the rich symbolism and visual imagery of the tarot as a tool for activating outward-facing intentions, to strengthen us in our self-understanding, and to actively express love and care for others.

Tarot Interpretation can be represented by the Magician: The Universe gives you energy when it responds to your question during a reading. You take the Universal energy and make it into tools you can use to deal with your issues. The Magician reminds us of the tenet "As above, so below," meaning things that happen on one level of reality also are reflected in other levels. In a traditional reading, like the Magician we bring down the gift of Universal energies and make use of them to effect changes on our level of existence.

Tarot Activation can be represented by the World: During a traditional reading you can bring the Universal energies around in a circle, that which you receive and that which you send out. The inner and outer

worlds become one. Your self is linked with all things and you are an
active participant in the flow of Universal energies.

Intentional Tarot can be represented by the Fool: You are emitting your
intentions from your own store of Universal energy in blind faith that
you can have an effect on the world. Like The Fool's Journey, the energy
begins with you. Take a leap, select the cards face up, in the same way
that the Fool has their face up, send out your intentions like the Fool
with their arms wide open.

This book embraces the trend for using the pronouns "they," "them," and
"their" to refer to a person of any or unknown gender. This relatively new
convention is especially appropriate when studying the tarot. Even when a
card depicts a character as specifically female or male, any insights implied
by the card will be of use to and can be applied to anyone anywhere on the
gender spectrum.

CHAPTER 1
Interpretation: Reading the Tarot Cards

Most tarot enthusiasts never stop learning about the cards. Just as with any religious text or intricate novel or television series, people will continually notice new details and make new associations which help them return to the material time and again with fresh eyes. This might be because throughout our evolutionary journey we've been rewarded for finding patterns and correspondences in the natural world that have helped us survive. Similarly, it feels rewarding and exciting to go through a tarot deck or book, either brand new or one we're already familiar with, and discover new patterns and insights to the cards.

But as any fool knows, each journey begins with the first step. Maybe someone has given you your first deck or you found one on a store shelf that looked simply beautiful and really called to you. Or maybe you have a dozen tarot decks or even more. I had over a dozen books and tarot decks (… *well* over a dozen!) before I could do a whole reading without looking into a book for the meaning of at least one card. Besides presenting the basic steps of a tarot reading, one goal for this chapter is to help you feel comfortable about getting off book and being able to read the cards all on your own.

The main thing I'm excited about with this book is the Intentional Tarot concept presented in chapter 3. To use this somewhat new method of working with the cards, it can be helpful to be able to quickly flip through the cards to find the ones that you want to use. This chapter is intended to help you get to that point with the classic card meanings so that the Intentional Tarot ideas can be most useful to you. However, you don't need to be proficient at doing a traditional reading and get completely off book before you try the ideas in chapter 3. With Intentional Tarot, it's perfectly okay to select cards based only on the images that speak to you. Go ahead and take that card with the big overflowing cup because it feels good, or include the one with the tower breaking apart if that's exactly how you're feeling at the moment. Any purposeful method for selecting cards for Intentional Tarot is just fine.

Because of my learning style, I completely depend on the images on the cards to lead me to their core meanings. Your learning style may be different, and the images might not be the key to getting off book for you as much as they were for me. In this chapter I describe three types of tarot beginners with some hints on how to use your strengths to do readings without any books or notes.

The Importance of the Rider-Waite-Smith Deck

A crucial turning point in the popularity of the tarot came with the publication of a new deck in 1910. Conceived and initiated by Arthur Edward Waite, illustrated by Pamela Colman Smith, and published by Rider & Company in London, this deck is commonly referred to today as the Rider-Waite-Smith deck, or the RWS.

Many universities require all music majors to develop some level of proficiency in playing the piano, even if they want to major in the violin or bassoon or voice. Many culinary schools require all students to master the omelet, even if they want to be a pastry chef or work in a steak house. For the student of the tarot, I consider knowing the images that originated in the Rider-Waite-Smith deck to be of similar foundational importance. It doesn't have to be the deck that you do readings with, and you don't even have to like it or feel connected to it. But just like a bassoonist at a piano, you will probably find it helpful to have a basic familiarity with its symbolism.

Many of the fun and interesting decks you can buy are intentionally based on the RWS imagery, especially for the pip or suit cards. These are sometimes called Rider-Waite-clones, Rider-Waite-inspired, or Rider-Waite-type decks. (Pamela Colman Smith does not always get the credit she deserves for her illustrations.) Some RWS clones are based on Smith's original drawings, intending to be stroke-for-stroke copies, down to each stone, leaf, and fold of fabric. Examples include the Universal Waite and the Radiant Waite decks. Other RWS-type decks are mostly-faithful re-creations of the main elements, proportions, and general details. The Nine of Swords will show someone in bed menaced by nine swords, the Three of Cups will show three friends dancing. Examples of this style include the Hanson-Roberts Tarot and the Llewellyn Classic deck that is used to illustrate this book. Hundreds of RWS-type decks are available, and more are being developed each year. Knowing the RWS symbolism, especially for the pip cards, can provide a common foundation to jump start your understanding of the cards in many of the decks that are being published today.

Unfortunately, the RWS deck is much less helpful in interpreting the sixteen court cards. You really need to look at the details of each card to distinguish between the eight monarchs sitting on their thrones, the four knights on horses, and the four pages presenting their icons. Finding deeper memory cues for the court cards is one of the things I look forward to most when looking through a new deck.

As far as the major arcana is concerned, the RWS draws heavily from the images on some of the oldest decks we have available, including the Visconti-Sforza and Tarot of Marseilles. By their very nature, the concepts of the majors often lead many deck designers to similar imagery. The Hermit card will often have a lone person with a lantern, the Chariot card will often have some kind of vehicle being pulled (or not) by two beasts. This makes the core meanings of the majors easier to remember no matter which deck you use.

In addition to providing a foundation for remembering the pip cards, another advantage of the RWS deck is its near ubiquitous presence in tarot literature. Many tarot instruction books that are not associated with a specific deck (including this one) will use RWS-type images, often along with other decks in their examples. Pamela Colman Smith's images have practically become the *lingua franca* of the tarot world; some level of familiarity with these images can only help you in your tarot studies.

Getting Off Book

It seems to me there are three types of beginners when it comes to learning the meanings of the tarot cards, or I could say "deciding what the meaning of each card is *for you*," since no two readers will see the cards in exactly the same way. As anyone who loves to pore over a new deck or tarot book can attest, you will probably be tweaking your understanding of each card your whole life.

Textbook Beginner (The Thinker)

This person prefers an RWS-type deck and reading about the interpretations from one or more books or online resources. They may eventually include one or more non-RWS decks in their tarot library. They might become interested in the correspondences found between some tarot card meanings and other esoteric schools such as astrology or the kabbalah.

Unconventional Beginner (The Explorer)

This person prefers a deck such as the Thoth or another deck that differs to varying degrees from the RWS images and reading the book that comes with that deck or online resources. They may eventually include one or more RWS-type decks in their tarot library. And while correspondences to other schools of thought such as astrology and the kabbalah definitely exist in the RWS, other types of decks often make these connections a major focus of the deck's development and need to be studied along with the basic tarot meanings.

Personal Intuition Beginner (The Dreamer)

This person could be working with any deck, but they do very little study of the card meanings via books or online. They are guided or guide themselves to intuit their own meanings and insights for each card. They may eventually go on to study some of the classic tarot manuals that have been published, but they usually rely on their psychic intuitions first.

Each beginner will have their own way of advancing and perhaps eventually doing readings without the help of books or notes. It's important to find your unique voice as you develop a way to read the cards that works for you. Here are some things that have helped me, a Textbook Beginner, finally put my books aside and feel confident on my own. These hints will probably work best for the Thinker/Explorer types while the Dreamers might prefer to hone their natural psychic connection to each card instead.

- Get used to handling the cards. Practice shuffling them. Get some muscle memory in your hands so you feel comfortable with them physically. When you're at home, carry them around with you as much as you would your cell phone. Tarot cards are generally quite a bit larger than standard playing card decks and can take some getting used to.

- Sit at a table and put the cards into groupings. Put each number of the pip cards together and get a sense of what makes them similar or different. Look at the progress of each suit from ace to ten and see how the essence of the suit evolves. Compare the details on the court cards. Play with different ways to organize the major arcana that help you see the story of The Fool's Journey or other major themes that seem to appear.

- Look up the meanings of the first few cards that catch your eye in whatever resources you plan to use. Depending on your study style, you might have just one tarot deck companion book, or you may have one or more what you consider to be beginner, easy, or classic books that you find helpful and informative. These are often very effective sources for getting started with tarot. Dreamers might prefer to select a book with only a small number of keywords. Get familiar with how the book is arranged. Put some sticky notes at the beginning of each section so you can quickly find the cards you'll eventually be looking for.

- Start getting methodical about reading the descriptions for each card while holding the card in your hand and looking for details in the images. However, don't read about more than ten cards at one sitting. Put down your studies for at least a few hours; then if you come back in the same day, go over those same ten cards again. Theoretically, it should take over a week of daily study to get through all of the seventy-eight cards. If you get bored or confused it probably means one of two things: (1) that's not the right book and/or deck for you, or (2) studying is hard and sometimes just not fun but you can push on through if you work at it. I don't know how many times I've bought a new deck and read through the Fool and the Magician, maybe a few more majors and a few of the pip cards, then had to put the deck aside and move on to other priorities in my life. Studying takes time and attention.

- After you've put a good effort into studying all the card meanings, put the book aside. (Dreamers: you can jump in here if you prefer not to study from books.) Shuffle your deck and place it face down. Turn over and look at one card at a time. Try to *feel* what its core meaning is for you, based both on your recent studies and any personal insights you may get from the details in the images. A picture is worth a thousand words, so you don't need to think in verbal terms about the meanings. Refer to your books and notes as much as you want to. You should only do up to a dozen or so cards at a time, then step away for a while.

- Using pen and paper or a spreadsheet or your favorite document software, write down two or three words for each of the seventy-eight cards. These words can come from books and/or your own intuition. Having the information come out of your own hands to the paper leads to a different type of memory than just hours of reading.

- Can you imagine a photo you have of a favorite aunt or sister or goofy friend? When you think of or look at that photo, you can feel the essence of who that person is, how you feel about them, and what was happening right at that moment. That is the goal for linking the mental image of a card to its core meaning. Close your eyes and mentally go through the Ace through Ten of one suit, picture the image, and think of your keywords. After the right amount of focused study, this visual exercise will usually be enough to bring the feeling of your full core meaning to mind. When you mentally get to a card that you can't remember ("Six of Pentacles, what the heck does the Six of Pentacles look like?"), then open your eyes, check your materials and start over from the beginning of the suit. Work on one suit of cards for a few days, then practice a different suit. Do the same for the court cards and different groups of major arcana cards.

- You will know you are starting to get off book when you can mentally go through all seventy-eight cards at one sitting, picturing the image of each card (if visuals trigger memories like they do for me), and remembering your core meaning for it. I do this exercise maybe once a month and am successful about 95 percent of the time.

Several quasi-standard associations have been developed that can make remembering card meanings easier. Instead of remembering seventy-eight separate interpretations, we can get to know the general meanings of groups of cards and then easily combine them during a reading. Remembering the information in the following tables can get you a long way toward coming up with individual card interpretations. However, as with anything in the tarot, not all readers will agree with these associations.

Memory Aids for Suits

Suit	Classical Element	General Realm	Cognitive Process	Metaphys-ical Being	Animal	Apostle	Sphinx	Season
Coins/ Pentacles	Earth	Things, Money	Sensation	Body	Ox	Luke	Bull / Body	Winter
Swords	Air	Ideas, Information	Thinking	Mind	Eagle	John	Bird / Wings	Autumn
Cups	Water	Emotions, Relationships	Feeling	Heart (Soul)	Angel/ Man	Matthew	Man/ Head	Summer
Wands	Fire	Will, Passion	Intuition	Soul (Spirit)	Lion	Mark	Lion/ Feet	Spring

Anything that can be divided into four groupings probably has been associated with the four tarot suits at some point. You will see the four animals represented on the Wheel and the World cards, as well as two sphinxes on the Chariot. Personally, I use the General Realm and the Jungian Cognitive Processes categories the most when I think of the four suits.

Memory Aids for Numbers

Number	Keywords	Add Your Keywords Here
1 (Ace)	beginnings, potential, opportunity, gift, root causes	
2	choices, balance, partnership, duality, union	
3	growth, completion of a stage, creativity, results	
4	structure, stability, inward self, the end of the beginning	
5	loss, chaos, instability, the powerless seeking power	
6	collaboration, harmony, relationships, reconciliation	
7	reflection, assessment, independent action, chance	
8	progress, power, mystery, prioritizing, cause and effect	
9	transition, near completion, limits, patience, solitude, fate, experience	
10	resolution, completion, results, consolidation, fulfillment	

Again, not everyone will agree with these words; they are what resonate with me. After you have done a fair amount of study, you are encouraged to write down any words that seem appropriate to you in the grid above.

Memory Aids for Court Cards

Court Card*	Keywords	Add Your Keywords Here
Page	new ideas, receptive, optimistic, exploring, vulnerable, inexperienced, student, messenger	
Knight	active, responsible, on a quest, committed, energetic	
Queen	influential, mentor, supportive, persuasive, inner control	
King	authority, success, experience, decisiveness, external control	

*The court rankings go by several names in various decks. These are the rankings used in the RWS deck.

The court cards are often said to represent actual people in your life or those who have influence over different aspects of your life. Some tarot readers associate specific court cards with general physical characteristics that many people have, perhaps to aid in identifying who the card might represent for the querent. I never use this method when thinking of who might be represented by the court cards but prefer to focus on personality and behavior instead. And I think the court cards do not *always* represent real people; they sometimes appear just to prompt you to think of the qualities of that type of person.

Combining Memory Aids for the Minor Arcana

Once you can remember your words for these groups, it's not a big step to put the court/number words together with the suit words to get an idea of the card's meaning. Your interpretation of the cards should vary depending on many factors, including the question being asked and the position of each card in the reading. Here are some random cards, their combined words, and how I might use them in a reading.

Example Cards	Suit Keywords	Court/Number Keywords	Possible Interpretation (based on the RWS images)
King of Pentacles	things, body	authority, control	A person who has control over your job or apartment or health choices
Ace of Pentacles	things, money	opportunities	A financial opportunity is at hand
Seven of Cups	emotions	reflection	An emotional crisis as you try to reason out what you really want
Three of Wands	will, intuition	growth	Seeing if investments that seemed good at the time will reap rewards
Page of Wands	intuition, passion	new ideas, learning	Finding something to be passionate about
Two of Swords	ideas, thinking	choices, balance	The need to think through a decision logically can cause immobility
Queen of Cups	emotions	supportive, influential	A wise friend or mentor who you can turn to with your emotional or relationship issues

Study Aid for the Major Arcana—The Fool's Journey

There is not a keyword grid in this section for the Major Arcana because most modern decks, including the RWS and its clones, include the name of the card along with the illustration. The name of the card is most often a keyword to its core meaning, although some are clearer than others; e.g., "Strength" or "Justice" compared to "The Hanged Man" or "Temperance." Instead, I am including a grid that is intended to help you become familiar with the names of the cards, the order in which they appear, and some basic relationships between them. The overall relationship among all twenty-two cards is often called The Fool's Journey. While any combination of cards will include meaningful relationships, I think studying The Fool's Journey is specifically useful for a beginner. Chapter 6 includes an expanded and illustrated version of this information with room for you to include your own understanding of the phases of The Fool's Journey. Your life experiences will bring individual meanings to how you see the progression that the Fool takes to the World card and then how the cycle repeats.

I've made twenty-two stages of five cards, and each stage progresses one card further down The Fool's Journey. This allows us to see all the adjacent relationships. I would not expect a beginner (or anyone) to memorize the five cards in each of these twenty-two stages, but they are presented here as a way to get familiar with the card titles of the major arcana and which cards appear next to each other in the deck. I've used the RWS order, with Strength as 8 and Justice as 11, but for reasons we won't go into, some other decks will have those positions switched.

Stage	→ → Progress → →				
			Focus		
1	0. Fool	1. Magician	2. High Priestess	3. Empress	4. Emperor
2	1. Magician	2. High Priestess	3. Empress	4. Emperor	5. Hierophant
3	2. High Priestess	3. Empress	4. Emperor	5. Hierophant	6. Lovers
4	3. Empress	4. Emperor	5. Hierophant	6. Lovers	7. Chariot
5	4. Emperor	5. Hierophant	6. Lovers	7. Chariot	8. Strength
6	5. Hierophant	6. Lovers	7. Chariot	8. Strength	9. Hermit
7	6. Lovers	7. Chariot	8. Strength	9. Hermit	10.Wheel
8	7. Chariot	8. Strength	9. Hermit	10.Wheel	11. Justice
9	8. Strength	9. Hermit	10.Wheel	11. Justice	12. Hanged Man
10	9. Hermit	10.Wheel	11. Justice	12. Hanged Man	13. Death
11	10.Wheel	11. Justice	12. Hanged Man	13. Death	14. Temperance
12	11. Justice	12. Hanged Man	13. Death	14. Temperance	15. Devil

Stage	→ → Progress → →				
			Focus		
13	12. Hanged Man	13. Death	14. Temperance	15. Devil	16. Tower
14	13. Death	14. Temperance	15. Devil	16. Tower	17. Star
15	14. Temperance	15. Devil	16. Tower	17. Star	18. Moon
16	15. Devil	16. Tower	17. Star	18. Moon	19. Sun
17	16. Tower	17. Star	18. Moon	19. Sun	20. Judgement
18	17. Star	18. Moon	19. Sun	20. Judgement	21. World
19	18. Moon	19. Sun	20. Judgement	21. World	0. Fool
20	19. Sun	20. Judgement	21. World	0. Fool	1. Magician
21	20. Judgement	21. World	0. Fool	1. Magician	2. High Priestess
22	21. World	0. Fool	1. Magician	2. High Priestess	3. Empress

This layout invites you to review five cards at a time, as well as to focus on a given card and consider the Fool's relationship with it. Again, this process will probably work best for the Thinker/Explorer types. I would picture you Dreamers as being able to see your version of The Fool's Journey as a sudden insight, or perhaps you would not be interested in this concept in general and will have your own way of seeing relationships between the cards. We all come to our tarot understandings in our own ways, and it's this individuality of interpretations that makes working with the tarot such a rich experience.

The following steps describe a method for practicing with The Fool's Journey study aid grid. Chapter 6 provides illustrations and space to document your own understanding of the Journey.

- Place a stage's five cards before you and examine the details of the images.
- Develop a story of what the Fool might be experiencing in this portion of their journey. You might have different ways to envision and remember this story, either through simple phrases, or by picturing an animated adventure tale, or by bringing together scenes from your favorite movies or books that represent this stage of the Journey. Chapter 6 has illustrations of the five cards in each stage with ample space for your notes and insights on the Journey. It also includes my own take on each stage and thoughts on the Fool's interactions with the focus card for each stage.

- Read about the five cards in your tarot reference books. As I've stated previously, this book does not presume to be an in-depth source for traditional tarot meanings. It might be best to read about the cards in numerical order. If there is a section on keywords in your book, choose one or two that resonate with you and say them out loud for each card; i.e., "Star: hope, serenity."

- Pay particular attention to the center card in the stage, both its general aspects and how it relates to The Fool's Journey. Each major arcana card is featured as the focus of one of the stages, so whenever you are able to come back and study a new stage, you will be able to get familiar with a new card.

- On the next day (or whenever you can return to your tarot studies), lay out the five cards for the next stage. Four of the cards will already be somewhat familiar to you and there will be only one new card added at the end. If you have more than one tarot resource book, it could be informative to read about the repeated cards in a different book in order to get a new perspective on them.

As stated previously, an important step for me in getting off book was to be able to mentally go through the cards in order, see the image of each card in my mind's eye and thus *feel* my basic understanding of each card, just as we would remember many things about a friend in a photograph. I would recommend studying only one stage at a time but don't obsess about having anything memorized before moving on to the next stage. Work hard but don't get bogged down with this exercise.

Once you've become familiar with the cards, you can practice in your head whenever you are in line at the grocery store or stuck in traffic or otherwise bored. But don't always start off with the Fool. Tick through the fourteen cards of just one suit, or the sixteen court cards, or the twenty-two major arcana cards. If you get stuck, do a quick search on your phone (if you have one and are not driving), and start over from the beginning of the group. Practice and study are not always pleasant, but they are usually the key to mastery in any subject.

This section has provided many memory aids to help you do your readings without turning to your books for help. Besides feeling comfortable with knowing what the cards mean, you will need to practice expressing your interpretation of the cards in a reading. Help with this aspect is coming up later in this chapter.

Some people can't think of the tarot without its obvious (to them) connections to astrology or other esoteric schools. Others may find those additional meanings frustratingly complicated. You will have to decide if you want to include other esoteric correspondences like this in your studies as you try to get off book.

Reversals

When a card is placed so the image is upside down, this is called a Reversal. However, when we say upside down, we have to define from which perspective we are seeing the cards. When you are reading for yourself there is no problem, but this concept can be confusing when you are reading for someone else. Some tarot readers like to sit across a table from the querent and put down the cards oriented toward themselves while the querent sees the opposite orientation. In that setup, reversals will look upright to the querent. This is fine if the querent only cares about the reading and not which actual cards have appeared, but I've always found this arrangement frustrating. I want to see and understand the specific cards I've been given!

I deal with this issue in two ways. First, I always find a way to arrange how we are sitting and to lay out the spread so that the querent and I see the cards from the same perspective. Second, I don't read reversals. When I place a card in its position, I always orient it to be right side up. It seems like I still get all the information *I* need for the reading, even if it's only a portion of the symbolism that a different, more experienced reader could be seeing in the spread.

For those who wish to include reversal meanings in their readings, there are several pathways you can follow, or you can devise your own process. You could consider the meaning to be the opposite of the upright meaning, an enhanced version, a subdued version, an internalized version, or any variant that feels right to you. Many tarot books include the author's interpretation of reversals and there are even books devoted mainly to reversal interpretations.

The Querent and the Question

Most traditional tarot readings start with a question or at least with a vague notion of why someone is wanting a tarot card reading in the first place. This question can be specific or quite general. In fact, a lot of the friends and family I have read for have been so excited to get a tarot reading that they very often just decide to ask, "What do I need to know right now?"

In a traditional tarot reading, the querent receives the cards and the interpretation of the reader as a gift from the universe. (The querent and the reader can, of course, be the same person.) To me, the primary magic in the tarot is this gift of energy and insight that the querent receives through the synchronicity of the moment. The question being asked is the focal point for this gift and is the target of the universal energies.

Lay Out the Cards

An essential part of the tarot is how the cards are laid out, even if you only turn over the top card of a deck looking for quick guidance. Each card has its place in the focus of the universal energies. I think if someone were to flip over a bunch of cards with a greedy attitude of "tell me, tell me, tell me," the energies would be diluted or the gift might not even be present. They might end up with just a pile of cards.

When I'm reading for someone else, I ask them to shuffle the cards however they like as they "think of what they want the universe to talk to them about." Some tarot readers don't want others to touch their cards, but I like the querent to put their energy into the cards. I feel like it somehow starts to open a conduit for the overall energy or connection with the universe. The endpoint for that energy is the querent, so it feels right that the querent should have a physical connection with the cards. After they shuffle, I have them cut the cards however they like so that they are in control of whatever cards end up on the top of the deck. Then I pick up the cards and decide what spread to use, assuming their energies in the cards will guide me to the most appropriate spread for their reading.

Tarot spreads can include just one card, all the cards, or any number in between. As a beginner you might want to stick to just two-, three-, or four-card spreads in order to get a sense of how they can interact with each other. Chapter 5 shows some example spreads for traditional tarot readings as well as Intentional Tarot spreads that are unique to this book. However, even at the start of your tarot journey you should feel free to make up new patterns for laying out the cards with your own creative ideas for the meaning of each position. Once you have a certain comfort level with your interpretation of each card, it's remarkable to notice the greater depth of information available when the meaning of the card is multiplied by the meaning of the position. That being said, I almost always use my personal version of the Celtic Cross spread. The symbolic range of the positions in that spread is quite comprehensive, and having ten cards gives just enough information without the reading being too long or too short.

It's exciting when a character in a movie or TV show is shown using tarot cards and slowly turns the cards over one at a time. It's usually a bit theatrical and suspenseful. Some tarot readers like to bring this element into their readings and I have no problem with that. I prefer to put down all the cards face up and describe the meaning of the position as I put each card down. The friends and family I read for don't know much about the tarot and are usually curious about what is happening. I guess I like to show that I'm not just throwing down the cards in random places and making something up about their question.

Once the cards are in place you should pause, look them over carefully, take a breath, be mindful that the universe is bringing a gift, and then begin your interpretation.

Present Your Interpretation to the Querent

At some point in my college days as I was fulfilling my language requirement with Spanish courses, I might have felt comfortable with actually conversing in simple Spanish with my classmates, but those days are long gone. While I still remember a smattering of vocabulary, there is no way I could look someone in the face and conduct even a simple dialog. I am out of practice, and those pathways in my brain are no longer here. Looking a querent (or yourself) in the face and having a dialog about the cards in front of you is very similar to conversing in a foreign language. It takes a good understanding of the vocabulary and lots of practice.

In the same way that I describe different general types of tarot beginners, I think there are different ways that tarot readers prefer to describe what they see happening in the cards. I can only tell you how I approach a reading, from the perspective of a Textbook Beginner. There are excellent books that describe the tarot experience from a more psychic perspective, and I encourage you to seek them out.

Even if you are not off book yet, take in the full picture of the spread before you say anything. Compare the proportions of the different groupings of cards shown in the key word tables in the *Getting Off Book* section earlier. These include the majors, suits, courts, and numbers. The presence of several cups cards could indicate that emotions are running hot on this issue while many swords could mean either that someone is over-thinking things or that the querent should consider all the facts before moving forward. If there is more than one Five card, the querent might be going through an especially chaotic time. As you are talking about the spread with the querent, the appropriate direction should become clear to both of you.

When I read for friends and family, even after all these years I still feel like I need to prove that I'm not making things up. I start at the first card, explain the position, tell them the basic meaning of the card, and then describe how it seems to fit in with the entire spread. I progress through all the cards one at a time, then we talk about the spread as a whole.

This method works for me, perhaps because I am less psychic than other readers. People who I've described earlier as Dreamers will probably develop much more intuitive ways to relay what they are seeing in the spread as a whole. Just as people fall on a full range of psychic abilities, we also vary in our abilities to speak extemporaneously and find the right words to say at the right time. Both psychic and speaking abilities can be improved with practice.

The Magic of the Moment

It's in the nature of a traditional tarot reading that no matter what, perfection has occurred and the magic will happen. The particular combination of querent, reader, deck, cards, spread, setting, yesterday, today, and tomorrow, always calls forth the right energy for that moment ... even if you forgot the difference between the Three of Pentacles and the Three of Cups, even if you forgot to take out the advertising cards before you shuffled the deck, even if the querent is befuddled about their question or thinks they are testing you with some trick. The cards that the universe causes to be placed in each position and the words the reader uses to describe what they see will always be true for that querent at that moment.

The querent may say "I don't get it. I don't see it. That doesn't make any sense. That's not the way things are at all." You can continue to pull a few more cards (called "qualifiers") or look for more associations in the images. Ask them where they think the blockage is. But trust that the truth is being told, even if it's not being heard.

The exception to this is if you keep laying out the cards again and again for the same issue in a short span of time. Even asking the same question twice in the same session and looking forward to "better" cards than the first time (or testing to see if the same cards will reappear) will dilute the energies received in either reading. In anthropomorphic terms, the universe knows what you're up to and won't play along.

Even though it turns out I'm not very psychic and I don't bring reversals or astrology or the Tree of Life into my tarot practice, my friends and I are still blown away by how our tarot readings turn out. I keep getting confirmation that there is *something* more than *nothing* going on and that the universe is sending something into the process that I choose to call energy. And that the magic is real.

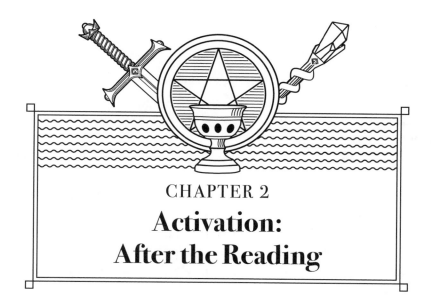

CHAPTER 2

Activation:
After the Reading

It took many years for me to get serious about my tarot studies. After fifteen or twenty years of curiosity and toe-dipping, and another ten years of occasional periods of intense study, I wanted my tarot experience to be something much more. Sometimes it felt like the energy of the moment was just left hanging with so much potential being unfulfilled. For another ten years I mulled over my readings, trying different spreads, focusing on different aspects of the cards, trying different post-reading rituals, anything to push the energy of the reading back to the universe as something like a prayer or a call to "let it be so." Now I realize that's like asking the water to go back up into the garden hose and return to the house. A traditional reading is a gift from the universe and it's not in the nature of that energy to turn around and return. I cherished the gifts of insight I received when I read for myself. I was amazed by the magic of the moment when my readings for friends and family hit home and they received the gift that they needed to know or think about. But eventually I really wanted to *do* something about all those options and ideas and insights I'd been given.

In this chapter, I hope to describe how we can project some of our own energy back to the universe after a traditional tarot reading. It isn't the same energy, like water flowing back into a garden hose; it is our own creation. Any time we want to make something better, the universe is made better because the universe is made up of everything. I consider this cycle of energy returning to the universe via specifically selected tarot cards to be an untapped source of universal good.

My suggestion here is to take an active step after your tarot reading but before you leave the table, with the goal of having your preferred outcome actually occur. However, I'm not suggesting this as an additional step to include as part of your standard reading process. The energy of the reading (the gift from the universe) and the energy of the querent and Reader should feel right in the moment for the cycle of energy to be completed.

After you've completed a reading, take a few moments to contemplate the spread, focus on the outcome you want to happen, and present it to the universe. Depending on your concept of universal energies or the Divine, you can consider this as a request or a prayer or as a metaphorical nudge on the great Wheel of Fortune. Look through the cards, both in the spread and in the deck, and select two or three that embody your ideal outcome. (The examples of card intentions in chapter 4 and the list of card theme words in the appendix can help you with this.) Focus on the cards and how they represent your desires, then release that energy with gratitude and hope to the universe or your deity. What's key here is that *you are intentionally choosing the cards by looking at them face up* and selecting them with meaning and purpose. The universe caused the cards that were important for the reading at that moment to appear. Now you can to use *your* energies to complete the circle and determine which cards to present to the universe as a step towards achieving your goals.

You may choose cards from the remainder of the deck as well as from those present in the reading itself. Since it's likely that you might want to use one or more cards from the reading, it might be nice to have a separate deck to select these same cards from so that the spread can remain intact while you focus on activating your intentions.

If the cards in your reading show that there are several options before you and you really want one of them to happen, then ask for that option to manifest. If the cards indicate that something is going off track, if danger or disease is present, then picture a better path and express your will that this new path should happen instead. As you look at the cards you've selected, verbally or silently express your preferred answer or solution to the reading that just occurred. If the spread before you has a most likely outcome position, then confirm or refine or change that possible outcome by placing a card or cards next to it filled with your will that *this* is the outcome you seek. In this way you are taking agency and participating in your fate before you even leave the table. Continue using that self-empowered energy as you take other appropriate actions in the following days, based on the advice given and the help requested in the reading.

Supplication and Manifestation

There are at least two perspectives from which to approach the activation phase of a reading. These depend on your relationship to the universe, the divine, your deity, or any metaphysical layers of consciousness that you understand. The different perspectives are primarily reflected in how you choose to articulate your desires to the universe. In the example above where I used the word "ask," you might want to use the *supplication* form of activating the tarot. In the example where I used the phrase "express your will," you might prefer use the *manifestation* form.

The supplication form might feel more comfortable for people with a background in one of the major Western religions. Examples of these in chapter 4 begin with the phrase "Please help." I try to avoid phrases like "please make," "please give," or "please let." Saying (or thinking) "please help" seems better because it implies that the person or people involved in the situation have their own agency and will also be taking actions toward the goal. Some examples of the supplication form are:

- Please help the workers protect the shoreline from the oil spill.
- Please help my pet recover from surgery.

Another way to phrase your intentions is to use the manifestation form as you focus on your goal. This form might be preferred by the non-religious in the manner of the *law of attraction*. In this wording, sentences often reflect the present tense of the verb "to be" such as "is," "are," and "am." We want to avoid pushing the intention into the future such as "I will stop smoking." The manifestation form of that thought might be "My lungs are healthy; I breathe only clean air." For the examples on the previous page, the manifestation forms might be:

- The oil is moving away from shore and the wildlife is safe.
- My pet is healthy and has fully recovered from surgery.

I've included both supplication and manifestation forms for the example card intentions in chapter 4.

At the Table

If you are the querent and someone else is reading for you, ask to spend a few minutes after the reading to send out your intentions of activating your preferred outcome. Do not touch their cards without permission but decide together on how to select a few cards that represent your intentions. Often there will be one or more cards already in the spread that will feel appropriate to the issue at hand. You could ask the reader to place them in a new position on the table for your moment of reflection. You might ask the reader to flip through the cards face up while you point out a few that you feel reflect your goals. Or you might describe your goals to the reader and ask them to look through the cards with you and help you find the cards that represent your preferred outcome.

When you are the reader and someone else is the querent, if the moment feels appropriate ask them if they wish to activate the energy of the reading they just received. Depending on the time available and your relationship with the querent, you could have an in-depth discussion of their goals in relation to the reading that just occurred, help them select a few cards that fit their intentions, then both of you send your energies out into the universe. Even without a full discussion, the querent might immediately know their preferred outcome. Depending on their knowledge of the tarot, selecting activation cards could be done in several ways. Whether the querent has a personal sense of the meanings of the cards or whether they would infer a meaning just from the images or their intuition, it's important to let them select the cards that fit their intentions with only minor guidance from you, if any. What you don't want to do is randomly pull a card and say, "This is your Activation card."

If you are reading for yourself, I'll assume you have at least a little confidence in your intuitions, interpretations, or resources for looking up the meanings of the cards before you and what they are telling you. In the same way as the two scenarios above, decide on your response to the reading, select cards that represent your desires, and direct the energy of your desires to the universe. You might wish to keep in mind the full cycle of the moment, from your original question, then to the cards and energy you received in the reading, then to the cards and energy you are projecting out with your activation. In chapter 3, I revisit these ideas for selecting cards that will activate the tarot energies.

Bringing the energy of a tarot reading around and sending it full-circle to the universe can be a rewarding experience, even if you don't focus your intentions on any specific goals. Many people make it a practice to close their readings with a moment of silent gratitude and contemplation. If you include an activation step in your readings, you may also wish to develop your own post-activation ritual that brings a sense of calming closure to the full energy cycle.

Practice Making Decisions

If you have difficulty in deciding where to focus your activation energies, you're not alone. I understand many professional readers speak regularly with the same clients who bring up the same issues time after time, but who never make a move in any helpful direction. If you keep asking for the same reading repeatedly, it might be helpful to consider your relationship to the issue. Does it feel like this issue defines you and that if it were resolved you would no longer be the same person? You should consider if you are more interested in the solution or the struggle.

Sometimes it's truly difficult to decide what to do with the information in a reading. However, it's important to know that for any option in life—even if you can't decide on a path—you are still on a path toward an outcome. Not making a decision is actually a decision in itself. Adding an activation phase to your tarot readings can help you practice deciding what it is you really want, as well as giving you the immediate experience of taking that first step on your own path. Decision-making is like a muscle—it can benefit from exercise. Consider the options you see in the reading and choose a direction. Don't worry about being "right" or the road not taken; trust the universe to make course corrections for the general good.

However, and this might sound contradictory, it's also important to approach your decisions about activation with a good understanding of your current mental and emotional energies. Try to become aware of the stories that you tell yourself that may be blocking you from making good choices. As Barbara Moore says in *Modern Guide to Energy Clearing*, it's a "sad truth that sometimes things that feel so good to our wounded child are not good for us. Rather than having a root cause, mental misdirection is usually a habit developed to support behaviors that divide us from our true ideals." In the end, even if we let our wounded child ask for something that is not helpful to us, I feel we can trust the universal energies to find a pathway to the general good. And taking the first step is often the hardest part of a journey. Once you've acted, taking more steps and adjusting your course become easier.

Proactive Activation

If you have a goal that you would like to put forth to the universe, you don't have to wait to find someone to give you a reading. You can begin a reading for yourself for the express purpose of laying down the activation cards you have in mind and sending out the energies to manifest the outcomes you desire in your life.

Look at the list of common types of tarot readings that follow. You probably have hopes and dreams for many of these topics, not only for yourself but for friends and family, too. You can practice both your tarot reading and your tarot activation by doing readings on a few topics every day. This will fill your week with cycles of energy, from the universe to you and from you to the universe, as you put forth your desires for many of these topics.

- Relationships: love, romance, friendships, partnerships, family dynamics
- Finances: work or other sources of income, career, major purchases, making ends meet, clarification on major influences

- Health: specific concerns, upcoming procedures, general healing, improving habits
- Recreation: vacation plans, work life balance, finding joy
- Inner World: spirituality, self-understanding, life transitions, working through grief, looking for fresh insights, manifesting dreams

It feels to me that all traditional tarot readings are some version of a request to "help me know what to do" or "tell me what's going on" in relation to the question at hand. Coming at a traditional reading from the perspective that you already know what outcome you desire will make an amazing difference in how you will interpret the cards, and even in the actual cards that the universal energies will cause to appear in the spread. The cycle of energies involved will be flowing full circle from the beginning, making the cards you receive and the cards you send out even more meaningful.

CHAPTER 3

Intention: Intentional Tarot

We can take the concept from the previous chapter of *Proactive Activation* one step further and skip the traditional tarot reading altogether. I call this Intentional Tarot.

In a traditional tarot reading, the querent wants to *learn* something of benefit to their question at hand. In Intentional Tarot, we want to *do* something of benefit to someone or some situation. Instead of beginning with a question, we begin with a solution. We envision exactly what we want to manifest, to alter, or to protect. Cards are selected face up with clear intentions. Our focus, as we look at and contemplate the cards, is not to interpret their meaning but to project our understanding of their meaning outward with intention to the universe or whatever deity you may relate to.

We practice Intentional Tarot in the belief that we are actually nudging the course of the universe. We are tangible bits of the universe. Our actions *are* the universe acting. Our actions may be just a pebble tossed in a stream or a butterfly's wings in the breeze, yet when you use Intentional Tarot you are being an active force that is influencing the course of the universe's unfolding. While the querent gets a response in the time it takes to lay down the cards and listen to the reading, with Intentional Tarot we act without expecting an immediate return. We are casting a pebble into a stream, which might possibly change the course of a river. Yet it is an action with a goal.

Where Is the Universe?

I use the phrase "sending energy out to the universe" often in this book. These words shouldn't give the impression that the energies are going out far away among the stars. Perhaps there is a similar misconception if someone pictures Heaven as being far away up in the sky and beyond the clouds. In this section I want to briefly describe a quick mental exercise that I hope illustrates the concept of the word "universe" as it is used in this book.

First, we might picture the universe as all the stars in the night sky. However, this image is too cold and distant to represent the intimate energies we feel when we work with the tarot. Gradually we bring the sense of the universe closer. Picture a universal boundary floating above the Earth's atmosphere, then picture a layer of universe settling down right at the cloud level. Next, the edge of the universe extends to the roof of your house or apartment. Then imagine it as suspended just below the ceiling of whatever room you might be in. Look up! The universe hovers there, only a few feet away. Then imagine the edge of the universe suddenly flowing over you and reaching down to the center of the earth. The universe is all around us and within us. It grounds us and makes us all a part of one unified field of energy.

When I activate the tarot and send energies out, I sometimes picture them as glowing all around me, extending from my heart directly and physically to both the object of my current goal and to the people or things that can influence the outcome I'm seeking. The universe connects all of us into one thing.

The same is true for the energies that come to us from the universe in a traditional tarot reading. We are receiving energy and information related to our questions, but the source is all around us and within us, not even inches away. As they say in the movies, the call is coming from inside the house.

Vocabulary

As with any new concept or procedure, we need new words and phrases to use when we talk about it.

Precant: I use this word to refer to the person selecting cards and sending intentions out to the universe. I selected this word because it ends in -*nt* like querent and has a similar-if-opposite meaning to that word. Querent means "one who seeks" and precant is an old, rarely used word that technically means "one who prays." While not everyone would consider sending out energies to the universe as a prayer, in many ways it could be seen as such, and so I thought the word could be appropriated for this purpose in an Intentional Tarot context.

Spread: Obviously, this is not a new word to the tarot community. However, I'm adding slightly to its meaning for the sake of communicating about Intentional Tarot. In this chapter I'm using "spread" in places where I might use "reading" when talking about traditional tarot concepts. In traditional tarot, the event that involves laying out cards and drawing an interpretation from them is called a reading. In Intentional Tarot, the event that involves laying out the cards and sending out intentions to the universe is called a spread. The word is used here with two meanings at the same time. The first is in the way that tarot folk use "spread" to mean laying out the cards. The second is in its normal verb form meaning "to open out something" as in "spread the news," or "spread your arms," or "spread the peanut butter." We are spreading or extending our intentions out to the universe.

To summarize:

- In traditional tarot we have a reader and a querent (which could be the same person) receiving energies from the universe. They "do a reading" with randomly selected cards and interpret the meanings found in them.

- In Intentional Tarot we have a precant (sometimes more than one) who is sending out their energy to the universe. They "do a spread" with deliberately selected cards and their intention is to influence how the universe unfolds.

Change, Protection, and Manifestation

In a twist on a traditional reading where we start with a question, with Intentional Tarot we will start with an answer. If you were to ask a question in a reading, what would you want the answer to be? Start with a mental picture of that goal being manifest, instead of asking for information and advice about it. This can be a proactive approach to personal concerns and can help you feel more in charge of your own destiny.

The domain of Intentional Tarot, however, is much broader than the types of questions we might ask at a traditional reading. In addition to the querent-focused topics listed at the end of the previous chapter, Intentional Tarot expands the influence of our energies to a much larger scale. In a traditional reading we could ask questions about a threatening situation such as a forest fire, but with Intentional Tarot we can proactively send energy and protection to those involved in controlling the fire. From breaking news events to general cultural shifts to planetary concerns, we can be active on a national and global scale, even if it feels like we're just a tiny spark in the distance.

Practicing Intentional Tarot in order to benefit someone or something often comes down to sending out energy for change, protection, or manifestation. Sometimes things are not going well, so we want to change them for the better. Examples of this might be sending out intentions for improved health or greater cooperation and peace between conflicting groups. At other times things are good or perhaps are in a precarious situation. In those cases, we want to protect them from harm or from conditions getting any worse. An example of this would be asking for safe travels for an upcoming road trip. We also might want to manifest something new or positive in our lives. This could mean sending out intentions to attract a romantic relationship or to do well at a presentation or job interview.

Intentional Tarot often involves specific everyday, real-world concerns. Most parents want their children to work hard and be successful. Many of the specific examples in chapter 4 reflect parental good intentions. Our concerns for those we love are broad, sometimes to the point of being busybodies. What if our desires and the things we ask for don't match with the desires of those we are concerned about? In that case, I think we have to assume that our good intentions will be conveyed to the universe, even if the details about the outcome may change. Intentional Tarot can be used anytime you are wishing someone well.

Many people in the tarot community agree that we shouldn't do traditional readings about other people without their permission; "Will Pat and Chris get married?" I would suggest that you also shouldn't focus your Intentional Tarot energies on specific outcomes like this either. Expressing a goal like "please make Pat fall in love with me" would be improper. However, I think a goal structured as "please help open my life to romantic love" would be in the appropriate spirit.

Select the Cards

When we purposely select cards for a spread, we are taking an active step toward our goal and claiming our agency in the situation at hand. The deck you use for Intentional Tarot spreads is important because you need to feel connected to the images and determine the role of each card in what you are about to do. (I will use the word "you" here but if you are helping another precant with a spread, you should just guide them in selecting their cards for their goals.) Each card selected must mean something to you related to the situation or to how you are feeling about it. Selecting cards based solely on the images is perfectly fine as long as they mean something to you in that moment.

Some example methods for selecting cards include:

- Use your psychic insight as to the meaning of the card.
- Consider the concepts and associations in the classic interpretations found in your favorite resource materials. The example intentions in chapter 4 and the card theme words in the appendix can help with this.
- Choose based on an immediate gut response to the image on the card as a whole.
- Select cards based on elements in the image. For example, you could pick out all the cards that have a cat or a lion in them, regardless of the classic meanings of the cards. Or if the woman in the Strength card looks like the person you are concerned about, you can forget about the lion and the title of the card and just focus on her.

As long as there is nothing random about how you are selecting the cards, you will be presenting the universe with your own energy and your own creation. You can select the cards by fanning them out face up to see them all at once, or by looking through them one at a time, or by any other non-random method that works for you. Be mindful that this is *your* effort and *your* action.

You will probably find yourself frequently choosing many of the same cards for different spreads. Round up those kings and queens! Go for those aces! Ten of Cups, Ten of Pentacles, all the "good" majors are yours if you want them. They represent powerful intentions and can be useful in many situations. If you are using the Intentional Tarot spread described as follows, you may find yourself pulling the more "negative" cards for the "My Under-standing" position. That's where I often choose to put the Tower, the Nine of Swords, the Five of Pentacles, and so on. These images help me articulate exactly what it is I'm actively working on changing or helping.

In some cases, you may feel that you want to focus on more than one aspect of a certain card, or perhaps the imagery on the same card from different decks reflects your full intentions. You might want to pull that card from more than one deck to use in more than one position in your spread. For example, you may be activating Universal energies for a political leader whom you associate with the King of Wands. You could place that card in the "My Understanding" position to represent your impression of them as a person and as a candidate, then the same card from another deck in the "My Goal" position could be the focus of your will for their success in the polls or the election. A final King of Wands in the "My Gratitude" position could reflect your appreciation for the service they have already provided the community.

Because you will be choosing specific cards, you might want to keep a deck in order by major and minor arcana, so you can easily find what you want. Intentional Tarot might also be a good use for a majors only deck that contains just the twenty-two major arcana cards.

Lay Out the Cards

As with a traditional tarot reading, the placement of the cards in an Inten-tional Tarot spread will add depth to the focus of your intentions. The right card in the right position of your spread can help you visualize what you are trying to express to the universe.

You might want to begin by using a single card for your spread. Focus on your intentions, the images on the card, and how the meaning of the card embodies or enhances your goal.

The Intentional Tarot practice discussed in this book usually involves sending out energies to the universe for the benefit of someone or something. In a two-card spread, one card could represent the subject (perhaps yourself) and one card could represent the change, protection, or manifestation you are actively seeking on behalf of the subject.

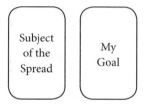

Moving to a three-card spread adds another dimension by allowing you to "set the stage" and clarify your understanding of the factors around the change or protection you are seeking. I find the "My Understanding" position helpful when I'm frustrated about something and want to express my frustrations to the universe.

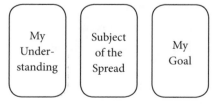

The four-card spread on the following page includes the concepts of personal actions and gratitude. In this spread, the "My Understanding" position would then include card(s) that represent both the subject and the background of the spread. For some people, including a promise for action will provide a sense of balance when weighed against the benefit we are trying to achieve. The offering or promise for action in the "My Promise" position provides room for acknowledging further actions or attitudes that you can contribute to the desired outcome in addition to the spread itself, something beyond "thoughts and prayers."

In addition, many traditions put an emphasis on thankfulness and gratitude. You can round out the Intentional Tarot experience by indicating something you are grateful for that's related to the spread. I have chosen to call this layout the Intentional Tarot spread:

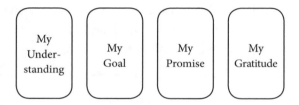

In practice, it can be difficult to choose just one card for each position. When I look through the deck, I tend to find several that fit my intentions, so I set them all aside until I have gone through the entire deck. Then I select no more than four for each position and place them in columns, but you don't need to have the same number of cards in each position. The card(s) in the "My Goal" column will be the major focus for the universal energies.

You don't need to fill these positions in any particular order. Often the whole spread will evolve as you go through the cards, feeling for the ones that seem to fit your intentions. Adding to your goals can prompt you to put down another promise card. Similarly, clarifying what you are grateful for can give you tools for enacting your promise. It's not unusual to keep refining the "My Understanding" position as you carefully consider cards for the other concepts in the spread.

Used separately or together, different combinations of these positions can themselves become different types. Some combinations include:

- My Understanding and My Goal: A brief spread for a desired outcome, with some background to help you visualize the full situation.

- My Goal: Just a single card that captures the essence of what you desire.
- My Understanding: When used without a specific goal, the card(s) in this position represent general good will for the people or situation you intend to represent here, almost as one might use a blessing.
- My Promise: Something you intend to do for your own betterment. That which you are focused on is implied by what you intend to do, such as selecting the Ten of Pentacles and sending out the intention "I will research life sustaining models for living on this planet in better union with it."
- My Gratitude: You can select cards that represent something wonderful in your life and radiate a grateful energy of thanks.

Chapter 5 has additional example spreads.

Reversals

As mentioned in chapter 1, in a traditional tarot reading, when a card appears in the upside down or reversed orientation, many readers choose to apply an alternate or adjusted interpretation of the card. With Intentional Tarot, the precant can choose to place cards in the reversed orientation as well, if that enhances their intention for selecting the card.

Since the cards are selected based on conscious intentions, it's not necessary to place them reversed as long as the card is fulfilling its role in the spread. If you are trying to manifest a bank loan, you might put down the Four of Pentacles in the "My Goal" position with your intention focused on releasing funds instead of grasping them tightly. If you are concerned that you are not working up to your potential, you might select the Eight of Pentacles in the "My Understanding" position to indicate your desire to start working as hard as the person on the card. In these examples, the cards could be placed upright or reversed, whichever orientation feels right to you for the meaning implied.

Present Your Intentions to the Universe

This step will be as unique for each precant as a traditional reading is for each reader. As with meditation or prayer, Intentional Tarot can be a deeply personal experience. How people communicate with their deity or other greater aspects of existence is often a private and intimate relationship. Like prayer, Intentional Tarot also can be done collectively. The participants, the setting, and the moment will all affect how the energies in an Intentional Tarot spread are released to the universe.

As you select the cards for the spread, imagine that your energies are charging up. I usually go through the whole deck and end up with a group of cards that is virtually crackling with the energy of the feelings and desires I want to express. When you place the cards in their positions, feel this energy leaving your hands as you let go of each card. Releasing the cards is the first step in releasing the energy of the moment to the universe. When all the cards are before you, look at the spread as a whole and continue sending out the energy of your intentions for the change or protection of the subject, or whatever it is that you are working toward.

How you proceed through the spread and how you communicate your energies to the Universal pool of energy need to be a purely personal process at this point. Your relationship to whatever will be receiving your energies will be totally unique to you.

Don't let an exhausted spirit prevent you from sending out your energies through Intentional Tarot. You may find that the more energy you give to the universe, the more you will feel coming back into your life.

Example Intentional Tarot Spread

I am thinking today about a good friend who is having surgery. I've looked through the entire deck and pulled out the cards that seemed appropriate. My goal is for my friend to heal from his sudden injury. Here are the cards I've selected for the spread:

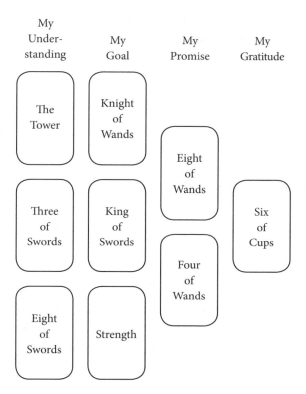

Below is my thought process for selecting each card.

My Understanding:
- The Tower: My friend's injury was sudden and could be life-changing if surgery and recovery don't go well.
- Three of Swords: The swords made me think of surgery and the heart says he is a good friend.
- Eight of Swords: This represents what I imagine my friend's wife might be feeling; distress with few options.

My Goal:
- Knight of Wands: This jumped out because of the red and orange colors and the feeling of movement. It felt like an intense battle was being waged with courage.

- King of Swords: My friend has always been a King of Swords type, and this also represents his surgeon.
- Strength: This represents the effort that will go into rehabilitation to get strong again.

My Promise:
- Eight of Wands: I will make sure to get updates from his wife, who is also a dear friend.
- Four of Wands: I will visit when appropriate and maybe bring them something to eat.

My Gratitude:
- Six of Cups: These people have been my friends for more than thirty years, and we have a lot of shared memories together for which I am grateful.

When I study the spread, I'm not reciting any certain words or phrases. I'm reflecting on the cards, and dozens of memories, thoughts, and impressions are running through my mind about my friends and the accident. But eventually I focus on the King of Swords card and just think "Please help him get better" for a while. I've left the spread on the table and occasionally refocus my intentions whenever I glance over to it.

Method Summary

The following steps can be used as a guide for working with the cards in Intentional Tarot.

- Focus on your intentions
- Select cards face up to present to the universe
- Lay them out face up
- Meditate on the full spread and on individual cards in their positions
- Send out your intentions however and to whatever you feel appropriate
- Close in some way that acknowledges the energies of the moment

I usually put the cards away with the main card from the My Goal position at the face-up end of the deck. Somehow this feels like the spread is sustained even after the deck is put away.

Actively turn the tarot tradition around and have the energy of the experience come from you and reach out into the universe. Remember that the universe is inside your skin and in the air you breathe; it encompasses whatever you are manifesting, changing, or protecting and all those with influence in the situation. In this sense, all things are one thing. Know that this is an *action* on behalf of the subject of the spread.

Being Intentional with the Tarot

This section will give you some additional ideas for using Intentional Tarot to nudge the course of the universe. You might need extra tarot decks for some of these ideas since the cards used might not be returning to their decks. This would be a good use for those decks you've collected that don't really resonate with you as much as others. Even if the artwork on the cards isn't your favorite, you can still picture the essence of the meaning of the card mentally as you focus on the spread.

Group Energies

Just as a march with hundreds of thousands of people united in support or protest of an idea feels powerful, working with Intentional Tarot as a group can elevate the energy of our goals. There are several ways you can work together as a group, including the following scenarios:

- A leader invites the group to participate and they articulate the intention of the spread. The group focuses on the leader's words, perhaps with their eyes closed, perhaps while laying out the same cards in front of themselves, perhaps while looking at the leader's cards being projected on a screen. The leader explains why they are selecting the spread and the cards. They talk about the spread or invite silent meditation if they feel moved to.

- The group decides on a theme and perhaps the spread to use. Each person pulls the cards that feel right to them and they concentrate on the same topic collectively yet individually. If the group is small enough they can explain the cards they selected. This can have the effect of compounding the general thought by hearing of intentions and solutions from different perspectives. This could lead to a lively discussion in general as people will often have differing understandings of and solutions for the situation. This could even be done on a coordinated nationwide scale.

Intentional Tarot with Movement

- Think of a card that epitomizes your intention. Arrange your body in a way that reflects how you feel about that card in your favorite deck. Create ways to flow into and out of that static posture as you focus on sending out your energies to the universe for the outcome you seek.

- If you are using Intentional Tarot for better physical health and are able to exercise or do physical therapy, bring a card that represents your intention with you on a walk or to the gym or to the therapist. It may feel awkward to keep track of the card, move it around with your water bottle, or have it in your hand when you want your hands free. But every time you put your attention on the card you can connect your desire for better health with the energies of the universe.

Constant Focus

- Some religious traditions use beads as a concentration focus for repetitive prayer. You can bring this intense focus to your Intentional Tarot work as well. Find three to five cards that represent your Intentional Tarot goal. Lay these cards out in a triangle or circle and concentrate on them one at a time consecutively and repeatedly any number of times that you feel appropriate. Additionally, you could use an actual string of beads and either look at the cards as you touch each of the beads or bring up mental images of the cards as you touch each one. Either way, you should concentrate on the essence of that card and why you selected it for your focus as you send out your energy to the universe.

- Think of a card that epitomizes your intention. Place this card in your home where you will walk past it frequently. Every time you see the card, focus on the essence of your goal. If you want to pull this card from more than one deck you can spread several copies of this card around your home. If you feel artistic, you can make a small representation of this card in your own style and spread copies of that in your home. You could even put a number, letter, or symbol that represents the card on small blank stickers and stick them all over your house. For example, if you think of the Empress card as symbolic of your desire to have a child, and there is a sticker with the letter E on your bathroom faucet, you can connect with the universe on this goal every time you brush your teeth. Or open the refrigerator or flip a light switch or pick up the TV remote, if you have stickers in all of these places.

Intentional Tarot with Art

- If a picture is worth a thousand words, then a tarot card is worth ten thousand. Make an art piece that invokes the cards that represent your Intentional Tarot goal. This may seem to be creating an extra layer of distance between you and your goal, but it can really help you think of small touches and associations related to your true intention, deepening your experience with the Intentional Tarot activity.

Intentional Tarot with Music

- Develop a chant or a musical tone that helps you mentally review the cards that represent your goal.
- Sing a song that fits with the cards you've selected for your spread. This adds an additional layer of nuance and meaning to your Intentional Tarot practice since the song interprets the cards and the cards help you articulate your goal.

Intentional Tarot in Daily Life

- A card that represents your desire for safe travel could be kept in the glove compartment of your car.
- A card that represents your goals for a better financial situation could be put in your wallet.
- A card that represents the goal of getting more focused on your studies could be used as a bookmark in a textbook.

- A card that represents sending out energies to attract more stability in your life could be hidden near a strong tree.
- A card that represents Universal energies focused on good medical test results could be kept with any paperwork you might be saving about your treatment.

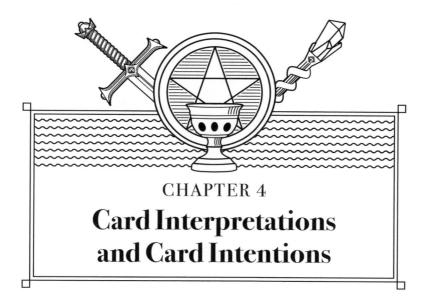

CHAPTER 4

Card Interpretations and Card Intentions

In addition to some basic keywords for the seventy-eight tarot cards, most of the information that follows are examples that illustrate some reasons or intentions you may have for selecting the cards to be used in an Intentional Tarot spread. In traditional tarot we seek to interpret the information that the cards are giving us in relation to our issue or question. In Intentional Tarot we use our own intentions for selecting cards to help guide our energies to the universe. The card theme words found in the appendix may also aid you in selecting the cards to use in your Intentional Tarot spreads.

The intentions that follow reflect hypothetical specific situations, but they use general wording intended to help you see how the card can be used in Intentional Tarot. Suggestions that indicate "my friend" could also refer to the precant, in the ironic sense of "asking for a friend." Suggestions that refer to "my child" are often more protective than one might use for a contemporary. Those that refer to "my organization" could be appropriate for any group such as a club, church, political party, non-profit, or for-profit company.

The examples are grouped by the four positions that, when used together, are called the Intentional Tarot spread. In that spread the My Promise and My Gratitude cards should relate to the topic of the My Goal card, which is clarified by the My Understanding card.

MAJOR ARCANA

The cards of the major arcana depict deeply psychological themes common to many people. Some tarot decks consist only of these twenty-two cards. A majors-only reading can be intensely personal and insightful.

0. The Fool

Interpretations and Keywords
New beginnings, taking a leap of faith, innocence, inexperienced, instinctual, fearless confidence.

Example Intentions Using the Intentional Tarot Layout
My Understanding:

The person I'm concerned about

- is an innocent beginner.
- is unaware of certain pieces of information.

- is starting on a journey or a new phase of life.
- is my foolish self.

The situation I'm focused on

- is more dangerous than it seems.
- is the beginning of a new cycle.
- has not been completely understood.
- involves spontaneous decisions.

My Goal:

Supplication form:

- Please help my friend have faith in themselves and their journey ahead.
- Please help me find the right things to say in the meeting with the "big wigs," to speak truth to power.

Manifestation form:

- Our new organization is getting off the ground and we are brainstorming our vision statement.
- My child has good companions that are helpful to them on their life-journey.

My Promise:

- I will approach this situation with an open mind.
- I will take a leap of faith.
- I will help others see the opportunities present in the situation.

My Gratitude:

- I am grateful for the flexibility to act in this situation.
- I am grateful for my guide and companion.

1. The Magician

Interpretations and Keywords
Willful action, resources at hand, working toward goals, potential, more than the sum of the parts, being capable, "as above, so below."

Example Intentions Using the Intentional Tarot Layout
My Understanding:

The person I'm concerned about

- can channel their energies into constructive outcomes.
- is a healer, teacher, or computer technician.

- knows how to make effective use of what is at hand.
- is my magical self.

The situation I'm focused on
- involves dealing with an intermediary who acts between our ideas and their actualization. A political or religious leader, etc.
- has many layers interacting with each other.
- requires many resources to complete.

My Goal:
Supplication form:
- Please help my friend harness all their amazing abilities and reach their goals.
- Please help protect our inner resources from being overtaxed by outside forces such as social media.

Manifestation form:
- Our political leaders are listening to us and creating rules and laws that reflect our goals for society.
- I am full of creative energy and regularly get into a state of "flow" when working on my projects.

My Promise:
- I will make sure my intentions are heard and my efforts are useful in this situation.
- I will take steps to make sure our cause advances.
- I will maintain the energy needed to deal with daily absurdities.

My Gratitude:
- I am grateful for the inspiration that has started me on this project.
- I am grateful for the resources I have available to me.
- I am grateful for leaders who use their power wisely.
- I am grateful for the earth, air, water, and fire.

2. The High Priestess

Interpretations and Keywords

Intuition, still waters run deep, divine wisdom, secret initiations, arcane mysteries, psychic energies, unconscious insight.

Example Intentions Using the Intentional Tarot Layout

My Understanding:

The person I'm concerned about

- is deeply spiritual.
- is a teacher, coach, therapist, spiritual advisor.
- is my secret self.

The situation I'm focused on
- is still evolving and changing.
- involves many unknown factors.
- requires the type of wisdom and insights you can only get through experience.

My Goal:

Supplication form:
- Please help my friend realize their potential.
- Please help me calm my "monkey mind" so I can meditate and/or sleep better.

Manifestation form:
- I am comfortable in job interviews and can express myself with confidence.
- The job candidates are all highly qualified and the interview process will go smoothly.
- The orientation materials for new employees have been rewritten and are helping people better understand the work.
- I have found a good listener who can help me understand some of life's mysteries.

My Promise:
- I will keep private the secrets I know about this situation.
- I will trust my intuition.
- I will seek out new experiences.

My Gratitude:
- I am grateful for my special place for silent contemplation.
- I am grateful for the wisdom of my teachers.

3. The Empress

Interpretations and Keywords

Maternal energy, motherhood, nature, fertility, creativity, generosity, abundance, sensations.

Example Intentions Using the Intentional Tarot Layout

My Understanding:

The person I'm concerned about

- expresses female energy, a mother, teacher, or community leader.
- loves the arts and creative experiences.
- is my motherly self.

The situation I'm focused on
- involves my ever-growing family.
- involves expanding our business in new areas.
- involves a young child or a new pet and gently teaching them how to behave appropriately.

My Goal:

Supplication form:
- Please help my friend during her pregnancy and delivery.
- Please help our manager learn to soften their style and be a little more relaxed in how they run the organization.

Manifestation form:
- My friend's art show displays their passion for their art and is a successful feast for the senses.
- Our concept for the new business is growing stronger and we are ready to give it our all.

My Promise:
- I will let my creative skills ripen and bear fruit.
- I will tidy up my living areas.
- I will connect with my children or the people I feel parental toward.

My Gratitude:
- I am grateful I have enough to eat.
- I am grateful for the mother-figures I have in my life.
- I am grateful for the time to gestate my creation.

4. The Emperor

Interpretations and Keywords
Paternal energy, stability, organized systems, traditions, authority figure, decisiveness, regulations, control.

Example Intentions Using the Intentional Tarot Layout
My Understanding:

The person I'm concerned about

- expresses male energy, a father, teacher, or community leader.
- is in law enforcement or the military.
- is a person in authority, practical, but not emotional.

- can be harsh and severe, perhaps aggressive.
- is my fatherly self.

The situation I'm focused on
- involves an encounter with the law.
- involves understanding how something affects the whole community.
- needs someone to provide stability.

My Goal:

Supplication form:
- Please help our leaders come up with just and equitable laws.
- Please help bring order out of this chaos.
- Please help us come up with a long-term solution.

Manifestation form:
- I am learning how to deal with my father.
- Our organization is operating efficiently, and we are following through with our plans.
- We have developed a system of just laws and rules; we are forming a stable, vibrant community.
- Our organization's leaders have created an infrastructure that encourages efficiency and prosperity.

My Promise:
- I will not let my emotions get in the way.
- I will participate in community activities.
- I will work with the powers-that-be to help create a prosperous social structure.
- I will analyze the information available and draw logical, practical conclusions.

My Gratitude:
- I am grateful for this period of stability in my life right now.
- I am grateful for the father-figures in my life.
- I am grateful for effective structures.

5. The Hierophant

Interpretations and Keywords
Institutional instruction, conforming to orthodoxy, following the rules, religious hierarchy, education, teachers.

Example Intentions Using the Intentional Tarot Layout
My Understanding:
> *The person I'm concerned about*
>> • is a teacher, spiritual advisor, or a bossy know-it-all.
>> • needs to listen to what people are trying to tell them.

- is very involved in their worship traditions.
- is a student of mine.
- is my intelligent self.

The situation I'm focused on
- involves that which I hold sacred.
- involves my house of worship, the leaders, and/or laypeople.
- involves someone acting as an intermediary.

My Goal:

Supplication form:
- Please help my friend understand what they need to do.
- Please help me be a good teacher.

Manifestation form:
- The intermediary is hearing our concerns and is presenting them effectively to the powers-that-be.
- Our organization is in touch with what our clients/customers need and want.

My Promise:
- I will be a good listener.
- I will try to conform to what is expected in this situation.
- I will stay true to my guiding principles.
- I will create a ritual to become more mindful.

My Gratitude:
- I am grateful for my educational opportunities.
- I am grateful for the traditions that have given me my roots.

6. The Lovers

Interpretations and Keywords

Having passions, making choices, sexual and gender identity, duality, part-nering. (I prefer to leave associations of romantic love and the beloved to the Two of Cups, but many readers bring these thoughts to the Lovers as well.)

Example Intentions Using the Intentional Tarot Layout

My Understanding:

The person/people I'm concerned about

- is someone I'm attracted to, either sexually or as a kindred spirit.
- is someone passionately obsessed about something.

- is someone struggling with gender or sexuality issues.
- is my sexual self.

The situation I'm focused on
- involves my current hobby or passion.
- involves my desires for sexual expression.
- involves making an important choice.

My Goal:

Supplication form:
- Please help me make this choice I'm facing.
- Please help people to accept me as I am.

Manifestation form:
- My partner and I are working through our issues and our relationship is becoming stronger.
- My friend has received many acceptance letters from schools/jobs and is weighing their options.

My Promise:
- I will be respectful of other peoples' choices.
- I will be honest and fair with my partner.
- I will carefully consider the pros and cons of my options.

My Gratitude:
- I am grateful for the friends who share my interest in nerdy things.
- I am grateful for the opportunity to have choices.

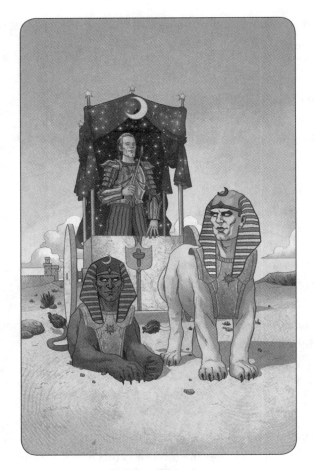

7. The Chariot

Interpretations and Keywords

Controlling with effort, willpower, transportation, movement, testing, self-control, managing dualities: emotions/logic, safety/risk, etc.

Example Intentions Using the Intentional Tarot Layout

My Understanding:

The person/people I'm concerned about

- is thinking about leaving an unpleasant situation.
- are at cross purposes in this situation.

- has a very strong personality.
- is my controlling self.

The situation I'm focused on
- involves conflicts and road blocks.
- involves modes of transportation.
- involves moving on to a new situation.
- involves trying to get something under control.

My Goal:

Supplication form:
- Please help my friend find a reliable vehicle.
- Please help me move past this blockage in my life.

Manifestation form:
- Our road trip is exciting, safe, and fun.
- We have strong, mature leadership who are uniting us and we're moving in a healthy direction.

My Promise:
- I will find strategies for a better work/life balance.
- I will react to immaturity by maintaining a mature attitude.
- I will help my friend move if they decide they need to.

My Gratitude:
- I am grateful for the transportation options I have.
- I am grateful for the amount of control I have over my life.

8. Strength

Interpretations and Keywords
Controlling with confidence, serene triumph, understanding and mastering your core strengths and passions, courage, resilience.

Example Intentions Using the Intentional Tarot Layout
My Understanding:
> *The person I'm concerned about*
>
> - is struggling with self-control issues.
> - has been suppressing their feelings.

- is being too aggressive.
- has a quiet and calming influence.
- is my powerful self.

The situation I'm focused on
- has gotten out of hand and needs someone in control.
- requires a peaceful, calming influence.

My Goal:
Supplication form:
- Please help my friend succeed at what they are struggling with.
- Please help everyone just calm down.
- Please help me find the courage to change the negative things I can control.

Manifestation form:
- Our new project manager has everything under control and things are back on track.
- I am remaining calm and respectful in this situation fraught with anger and bitterness.

My Promise:
- I will try to control my impulses in this situation.
- I will examine my heart for suppressed feelings and desires.
- I will be a calm and gentle influence for my child; I will be patient and understanding.

My Gratitude:
- I am grateful for my inner strengths.
- I am grateful for the calm compassion shown to me by others.

9. The Hermit

Interpretations and Keywords
Advice from a sage, guidance, retreating to find inner wisdom, introspection, productive solitude.

Example Intentions Using the Intentional Tarot Layout
My Understanding:

The person I'm concerned about

- is looking for guidance.
- is a teacher or therapist.

- is an introvert or loner.
- is my wise self.

The situation I'm focused on
- involves a conference or retreat that I'm working on.
- involves the need for wisdom and clear thinking.

My Goal:

Supplication form:
- Please help my friend be wise and confident in the life path they're creating.
- Please help me find the time to do some soul searching.

Manifestation form:
- We are confident that our lawyer is wise and mature in their knowledge of the law.
- I am comfortable with being alone.

My Promise:
- I will mentor someone who needs help.
- I will step back from the situation at hand.
- I will be guided by my understanding of the situation.

My Gratitude:
- I am grateful that I have a special place that I can retreat to.
- I am grateful for the wise counseling I've been given.
- I am grateful to hear silence.

10. The Wheel of Fortune

Interpretations and Keywords

Fate, imminent change, impermanence of sorrow or joy, the circle of life.

Example Intentions Using the Intentional Tarot Layout

My Understanding:

The person I'm concerned about

- is going through a rough time right now.
- doesn't see the long-term effects of their situation.
- is my lucky/unlucky self.

The situation I'm focused on
- involves looking forward to a change for the better.
- cannot stay this same way for much longer.

My Goal:

Supplication form:
- Please help us to find solid ground in volatile times.
- Please help me study effectively for my finals and get through this semester in school.

Manifestation form:
- My financial problems are getting taken care of.
- Our company's sales are increasing, and our finances are stable.
- The chemotherapy is working, and the side effects are fading.
- The old leadership has been voted out of power.

My Promise:
- I will remember that this, too, shall pass.
- I will not concern myself with revenge.
- I will work for a fresh start in our relationship.
- I will trust in the universe's pacing.

My Gratitude:
- I am grateful for this time of fun and joy, even knowing that it can't last forever.
- I am grateful for the consistencies I have in my life.

11. Justice

Interpretations and Keywords

Being judged, fairness, consequences, karma, putting things in balance, laws and policing.

Example Intentions Using the Intentional Tarot Layout

My Understanding:

The person I'm concerned about

- works at a law firm or a court house.
- seems to be judging me.

- is trying to straighten out a frustrating situation.
- is my impartial self.

The situation I'm focused on
- involves legal matters.
- involves gathering all the facts before making a decision.

My Goal:

Supplication form:
- Please help me to be accepted for who I am and not judged based on stereotypes.
- Please help me to have the wisdom to know the difference between what I can change and what I cannot.
- Please help this situation turn out fairly for all sides.
- Please help me develop an appropriate work-life balance.

Manifestation form:
- When work is allocated everyone gets a fair amount of assignments.
- There have been appropriate consequences for the actions of the people in this situation.

My Promise:
- I will carefully consider the information I see on social media.
- I will not take judgement into my own hands.
- I will accept that things usually turn out the way they should.

My Gratitude:
- I am grateful that the decision-maker is impartial.
- I am grateful that things usually tend to balance out.

12. The Hanged Man

Interpretations and Keywords

A new perspective, being in limbo, willing sacrifice, feeling detached or powerless, letting go.

Example Intentions Using the Intentional Tarot Layout

My Understanding:

The person I'm concerned about

- is facing a bewildering experience.
- is giving up something for others.
- is my confused self.

The situation I'm focused on

- involves a parent giving their time and energies to their child's activities and education.
- involves waiting for the repair person to arrive.

My Goal:

Supplication form:

- Please help me find the serenity to accept the things I cannot change.
- Please help my teacher get the most out of their sabbatical.

Manifestation form:

- Our project has been put on hold, and we've gained new insights on what we are really trying to achieve.
- The move to the city for my new job has gone smoothly and my partner has found a job they enjoy.

My Promise:

- I will face the inevitable with calmness.
- I will turn the situation on its head and look at it with fresh eyes.
- I will find opportunities to be of service to others.

My Gratitude:

- I am grateful for my moments of inner peace.
- I am grateful for the sacrifices others have made for me.

13. Death

Interpretations and Keywords

An ending that enables a beginning, loss, grief, complete transformation.

Example Intentions Using the Intentional Tarot Layout

My Understanding:

The person I'm concerned about

- is dealing with the death of a loved one.

- is afraid to make any changes.

- has left their past behind them.

- is my tired self.

The situation I'm focused on
- involves a time of change and transformation.
- involves something cherished that is lost forever.

My Goal:

Supplication form:
- Please help my friend accept the inevitable.
- Please help me make room for something new in my life.

Manifestation form:
- The company reorganization has allowed me to meet new co-workers and I still get together with my old group regularly for fun.

My Promise:
- I will not be afraid.
- I will let go of old thinking and old habits.
- I will allow myself to grieve for my loss.

My Gratitude:
- I am grateful for the hope on the horizon.
- I am grateful for having loved something so much.
- I am grateful to honor my past as I put it to rest and leave it behind.

14. Temperance

Interpretations and Keywords

Achieving appropriate measures in all things, harmony, the flow of actions that bring balance, moderation, grace.

Example Intentions Using the Intentional Tarot Layout

My Understanding:

The person I'm concerned about

- is a teacher or business analyst, someone who knows how to distill diverse information into an intelligent whole.

- seems to have it all together and to be living a balanced life.
- is my balanced self.

The situation I'm focused on
- involves two groups of people that need to work effectively together.
- is out of balance.

My Goal:

Supplication form:
- Please help my partner achieve a satisfying work-life balance.
- Please help everyone to reach a fair compromise.

Manifestation form:
- Our company is successfully combining being socially responsible with making a reasonable profit.
- My friend is good at presenting their true self, and their actions represent who they really are.

My Promise:
- I will carefully consider the proper response to the situation.
- I will work at controlling the habits that are holding me back.
- I will "walk the talk" and put my beliefs into practice.
- I will strive to stay on a middle path rather than take on extremes.

My Gratitude:
- I am grateful for the variety of experiences and interests in my life.
- I am grateful for all the elements that have combined to make something so wonderful.

15. The Devil

Interpretations and Keywords

Bondage to poor choices, being out of options, fear, hopelessness, lost independence.

Example Intentions Using the Intentional Tarot Layout

My Understanding:

The person I'm concerned about

- feels trapped, as if there were no more alternatives left to them.
- likes to play power games or mind games on people.

- has come to accept their unfortunate conditions as normal.
- is dealing with addiction or anxiety.
- is my wicked self.

The situation I'm focused on

- is one of great temptations.
- involves bad practices that have caused the project to stall.

My Goal:

Supplication form:

- Please help my organization find their moral compass and conduct business in a safe, legal, and responsible way.
- Please help me continue to live in the way that's most true to myself.

Manifestation form:

- My friend is treating their depression and is aware of the false stories they've been telling themselves.
- I am overcoming my fears and am moving past the blockage that has been holding me back.

My Promise:

- I will avoid the person who I know I shouldn't be flirting with.
- I will combat fear with humor and common sense.

My Gratitude:

- I am grateful for the treatments available for depression.
- I am grateful for my sobriety.

16. The Tower

Interpretations and Keywords

Sudden foundational change, a flash of insight into the truth, yanking off the bandage, useful stress.

Example Intentions Using the Intentional Tarot Layout

My Understanding:

The person I'm concerned about

- has had a sudden revelation.
- seems to need a new perspective about their situation.
- is my dangerous self.

The situation I'm focused on
- involves a natural catastrophe.
- has been mishandled for a long time.
- involves a relationship that has ended unexpectedly.
- is one where everything seems worse than bleak.
- involves a "bolt from the blue" that has left everyone stunned.
- involves something of long standing that is now over, changed, or destroyed.

My Goal:
Supplication form:
- Please help my friend learn the appropriate lessons from their misfortunes.
- Please just get this situation over with.

Manifestation form:
- I am confident in my decision to move away from my parents' religious traditions and am dealing with their reaction.
- My partner and I are pulling up stakes and making the move to a new city.

My Promise:
- I will be ready for the worst in this situation.
- I will accept the truth even if it hurts.
- I will let go of the walls I've built to survive so that I may learn ways to thrive.

My Gratitude:
- I am grateful for the finality of the change that has happened.
- I am grateful for the freedom of the blank slate around the corner.

17. The Star

Interpretations and Keywords

Hope, serenity, intuitions confirmed, clarity of understanding, wishes fulfilled, guidance.

Example Intentions Using the Intentional Tarot Layout

My Understanding:

The person I'm concerned about

- is a healer or a yoga or meditation instructor or student.
- is one of the calmest people I know.
- is my hopeful self.

The situation I'm focused on
- is one of hope in challenging times.
- involves my partner's aspirations and goals.

My Goal:
Supplication form:
- Please help my friend gain a sense of calm and peace in this situation.
- Please help our leaders be enlightened about the needs of the people.

Manifestation form:
- Our organization is recovering from the setback and is hopeful about our new direction.
- The surgery was successful, and we are hopeful for a positive, long-term outcome.

My Promise:
- I will be calm.
- I will have hope for a better day.
- I will speak the truth.
- I will shine without apology.

My Gratitude:
- I am grateful for the peaceful times.
- I am grateful for the guidance I've received.

18. The Moon

Interpretations and Keywords

Subconscious, possibilities, illusion, psychic instinct, dreams, confusion, distortion.

Example Intentions Using the Intentional Tarot Layout

My Understanding:

The person I'm concerned about

- is afraid to start over, to choose their next path.
- needs to see what their words and actions are reflecting about themselves.
- is my private self.

The situation I'm focused on

- involves a news story that is distorted, and the true events are being misunderstood by many.
- involves undeserved negative feedback or reviews of my group or company on social media.

My Goal:

Supplication form:

- Please help my child get over their night terrors and bad dreams.
- Please help me find the middle path between different voices that are trying to influence me.

Manifestation form:

- My psychic abilities are growing stronger every day.
- My partner is balancing their wild side with peaceful, private times with me.

My Promise:

- I will pay attention to the imagery of my dreams.
- I will be cautious if things seem too good to be true.
- I will face my fears.
- I will reexamine the beginnings of how this situation started.
- I will trust my steps when things seem to be unclear.

My Gratitude:

- I am grateful for my dreams and psychic insights.
- I am grateful that the situation is not permanent.
- I am grateful that I can see through the illusions and distortions.

19. The Sun

Interpretations and Keywords
Carefree joy, freedom, hope, vitality, clear thinking, self-awareness, enlightenment, optimism, confidence.

Example Intentions Using the Intentional Tarot Layout
My Understanding:

The person I'm concerned about

- is a child or has a happy, sunny personality.
- needs to see their situation more clearly.
- is my happy self.

The situation I'm focused on
- involves a fun, well-organized conference or work place.
- involves taking a vacation in a sunny place.

My Goal:

Supplication form:
- Please help us win the election.
- Please help this person experience more joy in their life.

Manifestation form:
- Everyone in the family is getting along.
- Our project is going great and everyone is working well together.
- My test results are back, and everything looks healthy.

My Promise:
- I will try to keep a positive and optimistic attitude about this person or situation.
- I will try to cheer up my friend.
- I will make each day a fresh start.

My Gratitude:
- I am grateful for all the happiness in my life.
- I am grateful that the testing is over.
- I am grateful for the success and growth of others.

20. Judgement

Interpretations and Keywords

Being called to act, being empowered to move on, renewal, change, inner awakening.

Example Intentions Using the Intentional Tarot Layout

My Understanding:

The person I'm concerned about

- is at a crossroads in their life.
- is experiencing a spiritual awakening.
- is my judgmental self.

The situation I'm focused on
- involves a cultural shift in progress.
- involves reviving a dormant idea or plan and making it successful.

My Goal:

Supplication form:
- Please help my friend understand what has been constraining them and see ways to make improvements.
- Please help me act on my urge to do something completely different with my life.

Manifestation form:
- Election Day is here, and people are coming out to vote in record numbers.
- My friend has survived their brush with death and is recovering.

My Promise:
- I will examine the things in my past that are holding me back.
- I will forgive those who need and deserve it.
- I will stop obsessing about a relationship that has ended.

My Gratitude:
- I am grateful for the inspiration needed to make important changes.
- I am grateful for the freedom I have to be able to make the transition that is ahead of me.
- I am grateful to hear the call of my Creative Unknown beckoning me.

21. The World

Interpretations and Keywords

Completion, achieving potential, perfection, self-actualization, coming full circle, wholeness.

Example Intentions Using the Intentional Tarot Layout

My Understanding:

The person I'm concerned about

- never stops moving joyously, and is a dancer or actor.
- seems to have every success they think they want.

- is a well-seasoned practitioner.
- is my complete self.

The situation I'm focused on
- is coming to a glorious conclusion, the culmination of an extensive effort.
- involves rewarding a person or group for their achievements.

My Goal:

Supplication form:
- Please help my child succeed and prosper.
- Please help my friend get that job.
- Please help my partner finish their book or other creative project.

Manifestation form:
- Our organization is fulfilling its mission in the community.
- What we have worked and longed for has happened and we are celebrating the victory.

My Promise:
- I will help my friend finish their project.
- I will learn from my past actions and make improvements.
- I will prepare for the next phase.
- I will serve the world using my talents.
- I will embrace a new integration of my skills, aspects, and needs.

My Gratitude:
- I am grateful for the successes I've achieved so far.
- I am grateful for a chance to begin again.
- I am grateful for the hard work that everyone contributed to the project.

MINOR ARCANA

The fifty-six cards of the minor arcana depict several experiences and emotional states that are common for many people. A brand new set of tarot cards is usually presented in order of wands, cups, swords, then pentacles. Many tarot books use this same ordering when presenting card interpretations. In this book I've put the cards in numerical order instead, to highlight the similarities and differences between cards of the same number.

Ace of Wands

General Associations

Number: Beginnings, potential, opportunity, gift, root causes.
Suit: Fire, will, passion, intuition, soul/spirit, lion, spring.

Interpretations and Keywords

An opportunity for a new creation, a successful enterprise, ambition, enthusiasm for a new beginning, passion, willpower, a time of great energy.

Example Intentions Using the Intentional Tarot Layout

My Understanding:

The person I'm concerned about

- is starting a new business.

- is optimistic, passionate, and ambitious.

The situation I'm focused on

- involves an unexpected opportunity.

- involves an effort that takes a lot of planning.

My Goal:

Supplication form:

- Please help my friend find the energy to get started (or restarted) on their project.

- Please help me make the most out of this opportunity.

Manifestation form:

- The bank loan has come through, and our business is getting off the ground.

- Our team knows what our goals are and we're eager to get started.

My Promise:

- I will humbly accept any encouragement from my coach, friends, and acquaintances.

- I will get on the ball and act quickly in this situation.

- I will support my partner's ambitions.

My Gratitude:

- I am grateful for the opportunities I have.

- I am grateful for the chance to influence this situation.

- I am grateful for the beginning spark from my muse.

Ace of Cups

General Associations

Number: Beginnings, potential, opportunity, gift, root causes.
Suit: Water, emotions, relationships, feeling, heart/soul, human/angel, summer.

Interpretations and Keywords

An opportunity for a new relationship or emotional experience, a spiritual awakening, creativity, understanding, a reconciliation that allows new beginnings.

Example Intentions Using the Intentional Tarot Layout

My Understanding:

The person/people I'm concerned about

- has just gotten married.

- is in touch with their emotions and interprets most things through an emotional lens.

The situation I'm focused on

- is a romantic or creative opportunity.

- involves a group that needs to get along better.

My Goal:

Supplication form:

- Please help my friend find happiness in this situation.

- Please help bring love into my life.

Manifestation form:

- My friend has found a good counselor and is addressing their depression.

- The new employee or committee member is a great fit with our team.

My Promise:

- I will ask this person on a date.

- I will surprise my partner with a little gift of love.

- I will reach out to someone who is sad.

My Gratitude:

- I am grateful for my passion about the art I create.

- I am grateful for all the happiness in my life.

- I am grateful for all the ways I have been truly loved.

Ace of Swords

General Associations
Number: Beginnings, potential, opportunity, gift, root causes.
Suit: Air, ideas, information, thinking, mind, eagle, autumn.

Interpretations and Keywords
A brilliant idea, a flash of insight, an opportunity to know the truth, mental clarity, thinking outside the box, power, reason.

Example Intentions Using the Intentional Tarot Layout

My Understanding:

> *The person I'm concerned about*
>
> • has a great idea for something new.
>
> • is sharp and clever, knows how to cut through confusion down to the core of an issue.

> *The situation I'm focused on*
>
> • is the beginning of a new school year.
>
> • needs to go in a whole new direction.

My Goal:

> *Supplication form:*
>
> • Please help my friend get accepted into the school of their choice.
>
> • Please help me figure out a solution to this problem.

> *Manifestation form:*
>
> • My friend can see the truth of their situation and knows what changes need to happen.
>
> • Our leadership is seeking out the facts of the situation and is developing a plan to respond appropriately.

My Promise:

> • I will seek out the truth and act on it quickly.
>
> • I will make sure my ideas are included in the final output.
>
> • I will speak truth to power.

My Gratitude:

> • I am grateful that a decision has finally been made.
>
> • I am grateful for the influence I have.

Ace of Pentacles

General Associations

Number: Beginnings, potential, opportunity, gift, root causes.
Suit: Earth, things, money, sensation, body, ox, winter.

Interpretations and Keywords

Opportunity for financial advancement, winning, good luck, tangible results, abundance, good things to come, a seed to invest.

Example Intentions Using the Intentional Tarot Layout

My Understanding:

The person I'm concerned about

- seems to be very lucky.

- knows how to cultivate donors or financial backers.

The situation I'm focused on

- involves a windfall or unexpected financial gift.

- could turn out to be enormously successful.

My Goal:

Supplication form:

- Please help my friend overcome their financial difficulty.

- Please help my child reach all their potential.

Manifestation form:

- Our organization's main benefactor continues to generously support our goals.

- I am taking advantage of the opportunity to meet with the person who is a leader in my chosen profession.

My Promise:

- I will humbly accept any financial help from my parents in this situation.

- I will be generous.

- I will act quickly on this opportunity.

- I will cultivate a healthy lifestyle.

My Gratitude:

- I am grateful for the gifts I've been given.

- I am grateful for the opportunities in this situation.

Two of Wands

General Associations

Number: Choices, balance, partnership, duality, union.
Suit: Fire, will, passion, intuition, soul/spirit, lion, spring.

Interpretations and Keywords

Gathering energy, choosing the next step, looking to the future, determination, raising your consciousness, making your mark.

Example Intentions Using the Intentional Tarot Layout

My Understanding:

The person I'm concerned about

- always has many ideas for our projects.
- is passionate about their vision and the ways it can be realized.

The situation I'm focused on

- involves our group making decisions for the future.
- involves gathering the resources that I need to achieve my goal.

My Goal:

Supplication form:

- Please help my child get the feedback they need from their teachers.
- Please help my friend get their new company or project up and running.

Manifestation form:

- Our organization is coordinating all the volunteers, and everyone understands how to discuss the campaign's platform.
- Our new manager has many good ideas and is bringing much needed energy into the office.

My Promise:

- I will take time to be pleased with my past work before I move on.
- I will make my intentions clear in this situation.
- I will balance my dreams with my ability to get them accepted.
- I will trust that my path is wherever my feet are.

My Gratitude:

- I am grateful for all the interesting potential projects coming my way at work.
- I am grateful that I've accomplished my vision for my recent project.

Two of Cups

General Associations

Number: Choices, balance, partnership, duality, union.
Suit: Water, emotions, relationships, feeling, heart/soul, human/angel, summer.

Interpretations and Keywords

Being loved, loving another, your beloved, close friends, emotional connection, partnering, harmony, connections, union and reunion.

Example Intentions Using the Intentional Tarot Layout

My Understanding:

The person I'm concerned about

- is falling in love.

- is excited about a new interest or hobby.

The situation I'm focused on

- is a wedding.

- involves a business merger.

- involves an event where friends from different areas of my life are together.

My Goal:

Supplication form:

- Please help bring a romantic relationship into my life.

- Please help my child develop good relationships with the teachers and students in school.

- Please help this newly married couple have a long and happy life together.

Manifestation form:

- My partner and I are working through our issues and our relationship is becoming stronger.

- My friend and I are finding more time to be able to do things together.

My Promise:

- I will do something special for my partner/friend today.

- I will keep my heart open to a new romance.

- I will welcome our new corporate partners with open arms.

My Gratitude:

- I am grateful for my love.

- I am grateful that my business partner is honest and hard working.

Two of Swords

General Associations

Number: Choices, balance, partnership, duality, union.
Suit: Air, ideas, information, thinking, mind, eagle, autumn.

Interpretations and Keywords

Thinking through a decision logically, over-thinking things, deciding not to decide, feeling conflicted, at a stalemate.

Example Intentions Using the Intentional Tarot Layout

My Understanding:

The person I'm concerned about

- is deliberately closing their eyes to the situation they are in.
- is feeling conflicted between what their heart wants and what their head knows.
- is overthinking the situation.

The situation I'm focused on

- has many issues and contradictions that need to be sorted through.
- is not progressing or evolving, is in a paralyzed state.

My Goal:

Supplication form:

- Please help me listen to my heart when logic is telling me what I "should" be doing.
- Please help me think logically when I'm overcome with emotions.

Manifestation form:

- The key decision has finally been made and our project can move forward.

My Promise:

- I will consider letting my guard down in safe situations.
- I will be patient and wait for the situation to resolve.
- I will decide not to decide.

My Gratitude:

- I am grateful for the extra time to think things through.
- I am grateful that the stalemate is finally over.

Two of Pentacles

General Associations

Number: Choices, balance, partnership, duality, union.
Suit: Earth, things, money, sensation, body, ox, winter.

Interpretations and Keywords

Weighing practical options, being adaptable, controlling an unsettled situation, multitasking, prioritizing, keeping everything balanced.

Example Intentions Using the Intentional Tarot Layout

My Understanding:

The person I'm concerned about

- is doing a balancing act with different areas of their life.

- has many hobbies and activities they enjoy doing.

- is transitioning from one job or home to another.

The situation I'm focused on

- involves a status quo that needs to change.

- involves something that is just about to go out of control.

My Goal:

Supplication form:

- Please help my friend make the best life choice for themselves in this situation.

- Please help my parents face the choices they need to make for the future with calmness and certainty.

Manifestation form:

- My life is in harmony with the universe and I am comfortable with the flow of events.

- Our organization is skillfully restructuring its finances and all the numbers balance.

My Promise:

- I will relax and enjoy the dance.

- I will ride the waves of whatever the circumstances bring.

- I will try to enjoy the variety of tasks in my daily life.

My Gratitude:

- I am grateful that my partner is being flexible about the situation.

- I am grateful for having choices available.

Three of Wands

General Associations

Number: Growth, completion of a stage, creativity, results.
Suit: Fire, will, passion, intuition, soul/spirit, lion, spring.

Interpretations and Keywords

Waiting for results, opportunities on the horizon, the law of attraction, expectation, foresight, seeing the big picture, awareness of potential.

Example Intentions Using the Intentional Tarot Layout

My Understanding:

The person I'm concerned about

- is good at attracting friends and supporters.
- is wise with investments.
- feels confident and secure in their place in the world.

The situation I'm focused on

- involves projects nearing completion.
- involves waiting for the results of an investment or a medical test.

My Goal:

Supplication form:

- Please help my friend exhibit the maturity and insight needed in this situation.
- Please help our group accomplish our full potential.

Manifestation form:

- Our organization is learning from past successes and trying new ways to serve our members.
- My child has completed her college application forms and is waiting for acceptance letters.

My Promise:

- I will practice "active waiting" until the situation resolves.
- I will consider the bigger picture.
- I will "keep my eyes on the prize."

My Gratitude:

- I am grateful for the chances to explore new ideas.
- I am grateful for the ability to see ahead.
- I am grateful to work with accurate and detailed plans for my project.

Three of Cups

General Associations

Number: Growth, completion of a stage, creativity, results.

Suit: Water, emotions, relationships, feeling, heart/soul, human/angel, summer.

Interpretations and Keywords

Friendship, fun, community connections, compromise, mutual support, spontaneous joy, celebrations, the ties that bind.

Example Intentions Using the Intentional Tarot Layout

My Understanding:

The person/people I'm concerned about

- wish they could get together more often.
- are the best of friends.
- are old friends from school.

The situation I'm focused on

- involves a joyful celebration.
- is our regular monthly game night or annual camping trip.
- is a time of intense happiness, even if temporary.

My Goal:

Supplication form:

- Please help our team/committee get along and perform well together.
- Please help me find a nice group of friends.

Manifestation form:

- When my adult children go out with friends they always have a designated driver.
- Even though things are changing, my group of friends remains close and communicates regularly.

My Promise:

- I will make the time to have fun with people I care about.
- I will get some people together to do something fun.

My Gratitude:

- I am grateful for my friends.
- I am grateful I have people to share this experience with.
- I am grateful for this deep moment of happiness right now.
- I am grateful for the arts.

Three of Swords

General Associations
Number: Growth, completion of a stage, creativity, results.
Suit: Air, ideas, information, thinking, mind, eagle, autumn.

Interpretations and Keywords
Heartbreak, rejection, learning something hurtful, ending in sadness, betrayal, alone-ness, pain.

Example Intentions Using the Intentional Tarot Layout

My Understanding:

The person I'm concerned about

- is very sad.
- is facing surgery.
- has been betrayed.

The situation I'm focused on

- involves something heartbreaking.
- involves unfulfilled promises.
- involves the breakup of a romantic relationship.
- involves something physically broken or dangerous.

My Goal:

Supplication form:

- Please help my friend find ways to balance pain with hope.
- Please help me heal my heart over the loss of my love.

Manifestation form:

- The damage has been done but we are dealing with it the best we can.
- I have let go of the thing I loved and am letting new things grow in the space left behind.

My Promise:

- I will accept this pain into my heart and learn from it.
- I will help my friend with the truth, even if they don't want to hear it.
- I will be there for my friend.

My Gratitude:

- I am grateful for the good times that often balance out the negative times.
- I am grateful for the transformation that came about due to my unfortunate circumstances.
- I am grateful to have loved someone so deeply that the ending hurts so much.

Three of Pentacles

General Associations

Number: Growth, completion of a stage, creativity, results.
Suit: Earth, things, money, sensation, body, ox, winter.

Interpretations and Keywords

Competence in a skill, master craftsperson, progress, teamwork, contributions, recognition for good work, manifestation.

Example Intentions Using the Intentional Tarot Layout

My Understanding:

The person I'm concerned about

- is a craftsperson, architect, or artist.
- is being observed, perhaps too closely.

The situation I'm focused on

- involves a multi-disciplinary group effort.
- involves a project that is not yet finished.

My Goal:

Supplication form:

- Please help my friend find a job in their field of interest.
- Please help our team communicate and work well together.

Manifestation form:

- The project is finished, and the correct people are being recognized and rewarded.
- The mentor program is helping people become highly skilled.

My Promise:

- I will give constructive feedback in this situation.
- I will listen to the advice of my peers.
- I will take steps to avoid delays in this situation.

My Gratitude:

- I am grateful for the constructive camaraderie at my workplace.
- I am grateful for the skills of our team members.
- I am grateful for the ability to learn, read, and study without distraction.

Four of Wands

General Associations

Number: Structure, stability, inward self, the end of the beginning.
Suit: Fire, will, passion, intuition, soul/spirit, lion, spring.

Interpretations and Keywords

Celebrating a group effort, happy gatherings, pausing to admire accomplishments, a wedding, a holiday, parties with friends.

Example Intentions Using the Intentional Tarot Layout

My Understanding:

The person I'm concerned about

- is about to be married.
- is planning a big event.

The situation I'm focused on

- involves people celebrating together; a graduation, wedding, completion of a course of medical treatment, etc.
- involves an event that has made the community come together.
- involves buying a house.

My Goal:

Supplication form:

- Please help my friend leave their comfort zone and find ways to meet more people.
- Please help me relax and enjoy the moment.

Manifestation form:

- Our wedding was a joyful event, everyone had a great time.
- Everyone I work with is getting along really well.

My Promise:

- I will encourage my friend to attend the party.
- I will watch my finances so that I can contribute to my child's wedding celebration.
- I will join the planning committee and help make the event a success.
- I will cherish these happy times, even if they are only temporary.

My Gratitude:

- I am grateful for the joy my club or organization brings into my life.
- I am grateful for my friends and family.
- I am grateful for my home.
- I am grateful for a strong foundation in loving my own life.

Four of Cups

General Associations

Number: Structure, stability, inward self, the end of the beginning.
Suit: Water, emotions, relationships, feeling, heart/soul, human/angel, summer.

Interpretations and Keywords

Dissatisfaction, a state of ennui, retreat due to weariness, apathy, depression, introspection, brooding on an interior world, bored.

Example Intentions Using the Intentional Tarot Layout

My Understanding:

The person I'm concerned about

- is bored and dissatisfied.
- enjoys spending their time with video games and other electronic pursuits.

The situation I'm focused on

- involves a decrease in customer interest for our products or services.
- trying to get people excited about something.

My Goal:

Supplication form:

- Please help my friend find something to spark their interests again.
- Please help me find a new idea to get my project back on track.

Manifestation form:

- Our organization has developed several new ways to engage with our customers/clients.
- My child is in control of their time spent in video games and is responsive to our efforts to try other interests.

My Promise:

- I will resist getting involved with another cause and will focus on my current efforts.
- I will resist going on social media too much.
- I will take a chance with something new.

My Gratitude:

- I am grateful for my imagination.
- I am grateful for being given options.
- I am grateful for the time to figure out the difference between what I want and what I need.

Four of Swords

General Associations

Number: Structure, stability, inward self, the end of the beginning.

Suit: Air, ideas, information, thinking, mind, eagle, autumn.

Interpretations and Keywords

Resting after stressful efforts, retreating from troubles, going on vacation, recovery, hesitation, drawing from reserves.

Example Intentions Using the Intentional Tarot Layout

My Understanding:

The person I'm concerned about

- responds to some things by withdrawing into their shell.
- needs to take a step back from some of the things they're involved with.

The situation I'm focused on

- involves a time of rest and recuperation.
- is on hold for now.

My Goal:

Supplication form:

- Please help my friend recover from their surgery.
- Please help our vacation go smoothly and be relaxing for everyone.

Manifestation form:

- The jury is deliberating and is reaching a just decision.
- I am enjoying this period of down time and trust that business will pick up again soon.
- My parents are enjoying their well-deserved retirement.

My Promise:

- I will take time just to relax.
- I will do some soul-searching about this situation.
- I will practice meditation regularly.

My Gratitude:

- I am grateful when I can have the house to myself.
- I am grateful for my inner wisdom.

Four of Pentacles

General Associations
Number: Structure, stability, inward self, the end of the beginning.
Suit: Earth, things, money, sensation, body, ox, winter.

Interpretations and Keywords
Trying to hold onto things, miserliness, stubbornness, self-centeredness, hiding money in the mattress, stagnant energies.

Example Intentions Using the Intentional Tarot Layout

My Understanding:

The person I'm concerned about

- tends to be rather selfish or to hoard things.
- does not feel secure.
- has closed themselves off from others.

The situation I'm focused on

- involves a hiring freeze or budget restrictions at work.
- involves a forgotten password or lost keys.

My Goal:

Supplication form:

- Please help my child learn to budget their resources wisely.
- Please help me protect my energies from outside forces.

Manifestation form:

- The bank is considering our loan application and will soon decide to release the funds.
- Our company is restructuring effectively and is working hard to keep all employees on staff.

My Promise:

- I will be mindful of my spending habits.
- I will delegate more responsibilities.
- I will know when to say "No."
- I will purge all that I do not use or need.

My Gratitude:

- I am grateful for the resources I still have.
- I am grateful for the control I have over my choices.

Five of Wands

General Associations

Number: Loss, chaos, instability, powerless seeking power.
Suit: Fire, will, passion, intuition, soul/spirit, lion, spring.

Interpretations and Keywords

Conflict, strife, simple competition, differing agendas, messy confrontation, internal battles, mind games.

Example Intentions Using the Intentional Tarot Layout

My Understanding:

The person I'm concerned about

- loves sports.
- is immature and doesn't yet understand the rules of society.

The situation I'm focused on

- involves a conflict that might not seem like a big deal but it's a big deal to me.
- involves a competition.
- involves Thanksgiving dinner with family.

My Goal:

Supplication form:

- Please help this situation unfold with fairness.
- Please help the dinner table conversation to remain civil.

Manifestation form:

- Everyone on the project is on the same page and is providing useful input.
- I have all the facts needed and am coming to a decision without much struggle.

My Promise:

- I will contribute my fair share to the group effort.
- I will listen to others' opinions with an open heart.
- I will not let petty arguments get under my skin.

My Gratitude:

- I am grateful for the energy of my team members.
- I am grateful for being able to play my favorite sports.

Five of Cups

General Associations

Number: Loss, chaos, instability, powerless seeking power.
Suit: Water, emotions, relationships, feeling, heart/soul, human/angel, summer.

Interpretations and Keywords

Blinding grief, loss, unstable emotions, frustration, solitude, regret, dwelling on the negative, unseen options.

Example Intentions Using the Intentional Tarot Layout

My Understanding:

The person I'm concerned about

- is working through the stages of grief.
- is exhausted from hearing so much unwelcome news.
- has been immobilized by their feelings.

The situation I'm focused on

- is sad and distressing.
- involves something precious that has been vandalized.
- involves an election that has been lost.
- involves a relationship that has ended in bitterness.

My Goal:

Supplication form:

- Please help my friend see that all is not lost.

Manifestation form:

- I am working through my sorrow and disappointment. I will soon re-channel my energies.

My Promise:

- I will accept that things are the way they are.
- I will look for reasons to be hopeful in this situation.

My Gratitude:

- I am grateful for the areas of stability in my life.
- I am grateful for the ability to weep.

Five of Swords

General Associations

Number: Loss, chaos, instability, powerless seeking power.
Suit: Air, ideas, information, thinking, mind, eagle, autumn.

Interpretations and Keywords

Defeat, deception, difficulties, dishonor, winning at any cost, unfair methods, humiliation, lost integrity, unethical manipulation.

Example Intentions Using the Intentional Tarot Layout

My Understanding:

The person I'm concerned about

- has caused a disastrous situation.

- has been cluelessly cruel, has made enemies.

- has been humiliated.

- has become discouraged and has lost heart.

The situation I'm focused on

- involves treachery or a defeat.

- is numbingly frustrating.

My Goal:

Supplication form:

- Please help my friend recover from their despair.

- Please help me learn how to overcome my self-defeating attitudes.

Manifestation form:

- We have studied the cost of victory in this situation and it factors in to our decision.

My Promise:

- I will be a gracious winner.

- I will carefully consider my attitude toward revenge in this situation.

- I will let go of all ways of being covert.

- I will draw strong boundaries.

My Gratitude:

- I am grateful that I've been raised to behave with honor.

- I am grateful to honor my integrity even if unseen by others.

Five of Pentacles

General Associations
Number: Loss, chaos, instability, powerless seeking power.
Suit: Earth, things, money, sensation, body, ox, winter.

Interpretations and Keywords
Financial or health difficulties, failure, despair, loneliness, marginalization, help is near at hand but unseen.

Example Intentions Using the Intentional Tarot Layout

My Understanding:

The person I'm concerned about

- is in trouble financially.
- is lonely.
- has been rejected by someone or by a job opportunity.

The situation I'm focused on

- involves the needy in our community.
- involves someone seeking sanctuary.
- involves someone's failing health.

My Goal:

Supplication form:

- Please help my friend find avenues out of their loneliness.
- Please help me overcome my financial problems.

Manifestation form:

- The refugees have escaped the war zone and have been accepted into a place of safety.
- My friend is facing their health struggle with hope and optimism.

My Promise:

- I will look for opportunities to help myself.
- I will send a contribution to a relief organization.
- I will help my friend in any way I can.

My Gratitude:

- I am grateful for the social safety net.
- I am grateful that my partner is sticking out these hard times with me.

Six of Wands

General Associations
Number: Collaboration, harmony, relationships, reconciliation.
Suit: Fire, will, passion, intuition, soul/spirit, lion, spring.

Interpretations and Keywords
Victory, celebrating someone, pride in accomplishments, being recognized for achievements, success, validation.

Example Intentions Using the Intentional Tarot Layout

My Understanding:

The person I'm concerned about

- has accomplished something to celebrate.
- is in the military.
- has survived an ordeal.

The situation I'm focused on

- involves a public event that many are excited about attending.
- involves someone in the public eye.

My Goal:

Supplication form:

- Please help protect the military and bring them home safely.
- Please help us win this legal battle.

Manifestation form:

- Our leadership is competent and working for the greater good.
- My friend is proud of their much-deserved promotion.

My Promise:

- I will celebrate my successes.
- When this project is over, we will have a party.
- I will be careful about getting too caught up in the moment.

My Gratitude:

- I am grateful for the efforts of those who work so hard for the common good.
- I am grateful for the support I've been given.

Six of Cups

General Associations
Number: Collaboration, harmony, relationships, reconciliation.
Suit: Water, emotions, relationships, feeling, heart/soul, human/angel, summer.

Interpretations and Keywords
Family ties, happy memories, a visit home, the feeling of simpler times, nostalgia, sweetness, innocent wonder, childhood.

Example Intentions Using the Intentional Tarot Layout

My Understanding:

The person I'm concerned about

- is someone from my past.

- is a mentor or person being mentored.

The situation I'm focused on

- involves a class/family reunion, birthday party, anniversary.

- involves a sweet gesture on someone's part.

My Goal:

Supplication form:

- Please help my brother(s) and sister(s) stay safe and healthy.

- Please help this home I'm setting up be a place of joy and happy memories.

Manifestation form:

- My vacation is relaxing and we are making wonderful memories.

- My friend has someone to protect them and stand up for them.

My Promise:

- I will connect with someone from my past.

- I will reflect on how my past is influencing this situation.

- I will give a donation in honor of someone in my past.

My Gratitude:

- I am grateful for my family.

- I am grateful for my memories of this person or situation.

Six of Swords

General Associations

Number: Collaboration, harmony, relationships, reconciliation.
Suit: Air, ideas, information, thinking, mind, eagle, autumn.

Interpretations and Keywords

Escaping a bad situation, getting help in adversity, achieving calmness, protection, taking a journey, crossing into a new world.

Example Intentions Using the Intentional Tarot Layout

My Understanding:

The person/people I'm concerned about

- is in mourning for someone or something.
- can't see what their actual problems really are.
- are refugees or immigrants.

The situation I'm focused on

- involves an escape or retreat from something troubling.
- involves a relationship that has become irreconcilable.

My Goal:

Supplication form:

- Please help my friend move on to a better situation.
- Please help the people who have been laid off find new jobs.
- Please help the refugees find acceptance and stability.

Manifestation form:

- My family is moving to a new home and a better life.
- The medical treatment is working, and we will be leaving the hospital soon.

My Promise:

- I will stay calm.
- I will cultivate a better attitude and leave my bitterness behind.
- I will help my friend leave their difficult situation.

My Gratitude:

- I am grateful for the assistance I'm receiving.
- I am grateful for this opportunity to move on.

Six of Pentacles

General Associations

Number: Collaboration, harmony, relationships, reconciliation.
Suit: Earth, things, money, sensation, body, ox, winter.

Interpretations and Keywords

Generosity, doing a favor, being helpful or asking for help, balanced giving and receiving, loans and scholarships.

Example Intentions Using the Intentional Tarot Layout

My Understanding:

The person I'm concerned about

- is generous with their resources.

- has imposed conditions on the gift they are offering.

- is finally ready to ask for assistance.

- has fallen out of favor, is being judged and ignored.

The situation I'm focused on

- involves providing for the needy.

- involves a grant proposal.

My Goal:

Supplication form:

- Please help my friend recover from the losses they have had.

- Please help me learn how to manage my resources efficiently.

- Please help our fund drive be successful.

Manifestation form:

- They have completed the paperwork and the materials we've been waiting for have been shipped.

- Our business is making a sustainable profit.

My Promise:

- I will make a donation to an organization related to this situation.

- I will not judge those whom I give charity to.

My Gratitude:

- I am grateful for what I received in the times I most needed it.

- I am grateful to have experienced both giving and receiving.

Seven of Wands

General Associations

Number: Reflection, assessment, independent action, chance.
Suit: Fire, will, passion, intuition, soul/spirit, lion, spring.

Interpretations and Keywords

Defensiveness, courage, facing a challenge, taking a stand, taking the high ground, sticking to your principles.

Example Intentions Using the Intentional Tarot Layout

My Understanding:

The person I'm concerned about

- is on the right side of the argument yet is still being misunderstood and attacked.
- frequently offers lame excuses in their defense.

The situation I'm focused on

- involves a confrontation.
- involves an organization that is fighting to continue to exist.

My Goal:

Supplication form:

- Please help us have the strength to keep up the fight.
- Please help my friend believe in themselves.

Manifestation form:

- We are confident in our stance and what we believe in.
- The person attacking me at work is backing off and our conflicts have been resolved.

My Promise:

- I will stand up for the person in this situation.
- I will defend my rights and the rights of others.
- I will determine where I can be of the most help in this situation.

My Gratitude:

- I am grateful for my advantages in this situation.
- I am grateful for having a keen sense of purpose and having something worth defending.
- I am grateful for the lively discussions I have with my partner about important topics.
- I am grateful for the opportunities that bring me to the growing edge.

Seven of Cups

General Associations
Number: Reflection, assessment, independent action, chance.
Suit: Water, emotions, relationships, feeling, heart/soul, human/angel, summer.

Interpretations and Keywords
Too many options, wishes and dreams, being tested, escapism, lost focus, mistaking fantasies for reality.

Example Intentions Using the Intentional Tarot Layout

Understanding:

The person I'm concerned about

- may be feeling overwhelmed about something.
- is a daydreamer or a conspiracy theorist.

The situation I'm focused on

- could end up with many possible results.
- involves an organization waiting for someone to make a decision.

My Goal:

Supplication form:

- Please help my friend understand what really motivates them.
- Please help this situation resolve in the best possible manner.

Manifestation form:

- The speakers we selected for the convention are all interesting and available.
- I have had several job offers and am evaluating my options carefully.

My Promise:

- I will contribute to the decision-making process in this situation.
- I will work to make my dream come true.
- I will regulate my consumption of escapist entertainment and stay involved in the outside world.

My Gratitude:

- I am grateful for the choices I have.
- I am grateful for what my dreams are teaching me.
- I am grateful for having many options.

Seven of Swords

General Associations

Number: Reflection, assessment, independent action, chance.
Suit: Air, ideas, information, thinking, mind, eagle, autumn.

Interpretations and Keywords

Betrayal, theft, unwitting stupidity, dishonesty, deception, guilt, being separate, cunning, strategizing.

Example Intentions Using the Intentional Tarot Layout

My Understanding:

The person I'm concerned about

- is acting carelessly, without a plan.
- doesn't fit in with the group, makes everyone feel uneasy.
- believes they have gotten away with something.

The situation I'm focused on

- involves a betrayal of our group.
- has not been well thought out.
- is illegal.

My Goal:

Supplication form:

- Please help my friend understand they are neglecting some critical areas of their life.

Manifestation form:

- The items that were stolen have been recovered and returned to us.

My Promise:

- I will be a team player in this situation.
- I will name the shadow in the room.

My Gratitude:

- I am grateful for being a part of a community.
- I am grateful for those who challenge me respectfully and truthfully.

Seven of Pentacles

General Associations

Number: Reflection, assessment, independent action, chance.
Suit: Earth, things, money, sensation, body, ox, winter.

Interpretations and Keywords

Evaluating our efforts, managing expectations, taking a break, making a decision, documenting, reflecting, "pause for the cause."

Example Intentions Using the Intentional Tarot Layout

My Understanding:

The person I'm concerned about

- always wants just a little bit more.
- is considering their options, deciding what to do next.
- isn't living up to our expectations.
- is reflecting on the work they are putting into their relationship.

The situation I'm focused on

- involves re-assessing our project now that we're at the mid-way point.
- involves deciding if we want to organize the big annual event again this year.

My Goal:

Supplication form:

- Please help my partner understand all the good they have done and how much they are appreciated.
- Please help me get my project to a point where I can take a step back from it.

Manifestation form:

- The building inspection is going well, permits are being approved.
- My organization is examining our workflow and we are making many improvements to our processes.
- The surgery team knows exactly what to do during the operation.

My Promise:

- I will help someone take a break from their tasks.
- I will examine my expectations.
- I will prepare for the next phase of the situation.

My Gratitude:

- I am grateful for my team's ability to get things done.
- I am grateful for having work I find satisfying.
- I am grateful for those who advised me to rest and be kind to myself.

Eight of Wands

General Associations

Number: Progress, power, mystery, prioritizing, cause and effect.
Suit: Fire, will, passion, intuition, soul/spirit, lion, spring.

Interpretations and Keywords

Events unfolding quickly, powerful influences getting results, rapid movement, now is the time to act, travel, messages.

Example Intentions Using the Intentional Tarot Layout

My Understanding:

The person I'm concerned about

- is on a journey.

- is coming into our project from outside the company.

The situation I'm focused on

- is evolving quickly; we don't seem to have much control.

- involves a message that could change everything.

My Goal:

Supplication form:

- Please help my friend know when they should take the action they are considering.

- Please help these sudden events have a positive impact.

Manifestation form:

- I have arrived at the airport with everything I need and the flight is on time.

- Everything is falling into place and the situation can be resolved quickly.

My Promise:

- I will be ready for whatever happens.

- I will give up the need to control the situation.

- I will reach out and connect with this person.

My Gratitude:

- I am grateful for the light at the end of the tunnel.

- I am grateful that things are progressing so smoothly.

Eight of Cups

General Associations

Number: Progress, power, mystery, prioritizing, cause and effect.
Suit: Water, emotions, relationships, feeling, heart/soul, human/angel, summer.

Interpretations and Keywords

Being guided by strong feelings, dissatisfaction, emotional stagnation, leaving the known for the unknown, seeking for something missing, a spiritual journey.

Example Intentions Using the Intentional Tarot Layout

My Understanding:

The person I'm concerned about

- is feeling discontented with their situation.

- is leaving our organization and starting a new job.

The situation I'm focused on

- involves a stable situation that needs some finishing touches.

- involves something missing that must be found.

My Goal:

Supplication form:

- Please help my friend have the strength to change their situation.

- Please help my child with their transition to college life.

Manifestation form:

- My organization is finding new products and services to offer our clients/customers.

- I am ready and eager to make the move that I've been thinking about.

My Promise:

- I will help my friend with their remodeling project.

- I will find ways to improve the situation at hand.

- I will quit my job.

My Gratitude:

- I am grateful for the freedom to try new things.

- I am grateful for this new situation I've found.

Eight of Swords

General Associations

Number: Progress, power, mystery, prioritizing, cause and effect.
Suit: Air, ideas, information, thinking, mind, eagle, autumn.

Interpretations and Keywords

Perception of danger, feeling trapped, lack of options, roadblocks, powerlessness, finding a way out, your own worst enemy.

Example Intentions Using the Intentional Tarot Layout

My Understanding:

The person I'm concerned about

- doesn't seem to notice some valuable resources they have.
- has been humiliated.
- seems to be repressed or restricted.

The situation I'm focused on

- involves a person or group that has been brainwashed into "learned helplessness."
- involves unnecessary road blocks which are hindering a project.

My Goal:

Supplication form:

- Please help my friend find a way out of their unpleasant situation.
- Please help those who are vulnerable and in isolation.

Manifestation form:

- Our group has overcome the impasse and is now progressing toward our goals.
- I have found ways to take agency in my situation and I am untangling the mess that surrounds me.

My Promise:

- I will reassess the things that I think are holding me back.
- I will help this person help themselves.
- I will take a stand and speak up for myself.

My Gratitude:

- I am grateful for the pathways available to me during this dark time.
- I am grateful for those who rescue others.
- I am grateful for all the times I have overcome my own sense of powerlessness.

Eight of Pentacles

General Associations
Number: Progress, power, mystery, prioritizing, cause and effect.
Suit: Earth, things, money, sensation, body, ox, winter.

Interpretations and Keywords
Mastering a talent, hard work, dedication, diligence, practice, patience, attention to details, pride in improvement.

Example Intentions Using the Intentional Tarot Layout

My Understanding:

The person I'm concerned about

- is diligent at their job, music practice, volunteer efforts, etc.
- is (or wants to be) a master craftsperson.

The situation I'm focused on

- involves a big task ahead of us.
- involves something that is mass produced.

My Goal:

Supplication form:

- Please help me be patient with tasks that seem repetitive.
- Please help my child learn how to do well in school.

Manifestation form:

- My partner and I enjoy working on our relationship and having regular date nights.
- Our organization is becoming known for the excellence of what we make or do.

My Promise:

- I will pay closer attention to details.
- I will keep working on this project.
- I will help my child organize their time so they can study/practice efficiently.

My Gratitude:

- I am grateful for having the tools I need for my craft.
- I am grateful for being able to concentrate on my interests.
- I am grateful to be able to make money doing the work that I love.

Nine of Wands

General Associations

Number: Transition, near completion, limits, patience, solitude, fate, experience.
Suit: Fire, will, passion, intuition, soul/spirit, lion, spring.

Interpretations and Keywords

Gathering strength after a battle, vigilance, stamina, awaiting the coming conflict, discipline, readiness, almost there.

Example Intentions Using the Intentional Tarot Layout

My Understanding:

The person I'm concerned about

- tends to respond defensively to many situations.
- feels beset by problems.

The situation I'm focused on

- has been going on for far too long.
- involves a returning medical condition.

My Goal:

Supplication form:

- Please help my friend be ready for what they are up against next.
- Please help my partner understand that they don't have to always be looking for a fight.

Manifestation form:

- Our organization is fighting the good fight and won't give up.
- My child and I are learning how to deal with our problems.

My Promise:

- I will consider if it's time to give up the fight.
- I will have courage in this situation.
- I will be ready for whatever happens.
- I will offer support to those in need.

My Gratitude:

- I am grateful that my efforts have made me strong.

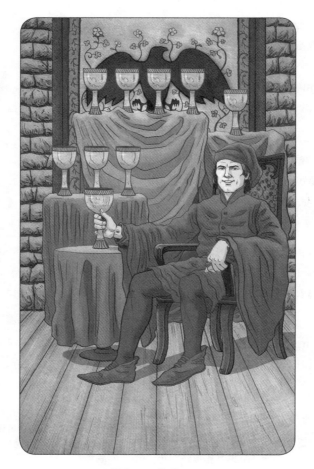

Nine of Cups

General Associations

Number: Transition, near completion, limits, patience, solitude, fate, experience.

Suit: Water, emotions, relationships, feeling, heart/soul, human/angel, summer.

Interpretations and Keywords

Good fortune, good health, happiness, extending a welcome, fulfillment of wishes, pleasure, emotional contentment.

Example Intentions Using the Intentional Tarot Layout

My Understanding:

The person I'm concerned about

- is a gracious host.
- is focused on achieving their heart's desire.
- enjoys going out and having a good time.

The situation I'm focused on

- involves the planning stages of a big celebration.
- involves our annual holiday gathering.

My Goal:

Supplication form:

- Please help my friend get what they've been wishing for.
- Please help me make the party I'm planning turn out to be a wonderful time for everyone.

Manifestation form:

- Our hotel is even nicer than we expected.
- My friend is enjoying good health and financial stability.

My Promise:

- I will take time to relax with friends.
- I will try to enjoy life more.
- I will invite people over to my home.

My Gratitude:

- I am grateful for the fun events on my calendar.
- I am grateful for having everything I really need.
- I am grateful for this time of contentment.

Nine of Swords

General Associations
Number: Transition, near completion, limits, patience, solitude, fate, experience.
Suit: Air, ideas, information, thinking, mind, eagle, autumn.

Interpretations and Keywords
Oppressive thoughts, worry, expecting the worst, nightmares, depression, vulnerability.

Example Intentions Using the Intentional Tarot Layout

My Understanding:

The person I'm concerned about

- is depressed, is focused on their regrets.
- is having trouble sleeping.
- spends a lot of time reading the arguments on social media.
- is being "gaslighted" by a cruel person. (Gaslighting means to manipulate someone by psychological means into questioning their own sanity.)

The situation I'm focused on

- seems inescapable.
- is all that I can think about right now.

My Goal:

Supplication form:

- Please help my friend forgive themselves.
- Please help remove the causes of all these oppressive thoughts.

Manifestation form:

- My friend understands what is going on and is removing themselves from the situation.
- I am in control of my thoughts and worries. I'm making them take their appropriate proportion of my attention.

My Promise:

- I will spend less time on social media.
- I will take some responsibility for this unfortunate situation.
- I will transform worry into wish.
- I will change my nighttime habits to improve my sleep patterns.
- I will make time to concentrate on my gifts each day.

My Gratitude:

- I am grateful for my parents, even when they worry about me too much.
- I am grateful that I can be forgiven for the careless words I said.

Nine of Pentacles

General Associations

Number: Transition, near completion, limits, patience, solitude, fate, experience.
Suit: Earth, things, money, sensation, body, ox, winter.

Interpretations and Keywords

Abundance, personal satisfaction, independence, attainment, in control of resources, self-confidence.

Example Intentions Using the Intentional Tarot Layout

My Understanding:

The person I'm concerned about

- is self-confident and self-disciplined.
- is financially comfortable.

The situation I'm focused on

- involves cultivating a rich environment.
- involves a garden, farm, or vineyard.

My Goal:

Supplication form:

- Please help my parents achieve the comfortable retirement they deserve.
- Please help me know the compromises necessary for the success I'm working toward.

Manifestation form:

- My friend is making good decisions for their long-term financial success.
- My organization has reached their fund-raising goals for the year.

My Promise:

- I will subdue the impulses that distract me from my path.
- I will not look for external validation of my goals.
- I will be self-reliant and confident.
- I will use my privilege or entitlement in service to those without any.

My Gratitude:

- I am grateful for knowing how to be alone but not lonely.
- I am grateful for being able to enjoy the fruits of my labors.

Ten of Wands

General Associations
Number: Resolution, completion, results, consolidation, fulfillment.
Suit: Fire, will, passion, intuition, soul/spirit, lion, spring.

Interpretations and Keywords
Feeling overcommitted, overextended, persisting with responsibilities, obligations, maintenance mode after a big project.

Example Intentions Using the Intentional Tarot Layout

My Understanding:

The person I'm concerned about

- is burdened with too many responsibilities.
- loves to have many irons in the fire, to be active with many causes and organizations.
- feels they are taking the weight of the world on their shoulders.

The situation I'm focused on

- involves a patient with difficult medical problems or their caregiver.
- involves a person who might not be handling their stress well.

My Goal:

Supplication form:

- Please help my friend decide what things they can let go of.
- Please help me walk the path I am on and handle the responsibilities I must bear.

Manifestation form:

- Our organization is effectively balancing everyone's work load.
- My friends are managing their financial situation effectively.

My Promise:

- I will try to take some responsibilities from someone who is overwhelmed.
- I will look for ways to be better organized and efficient.
- I will step back from some of my involvements.
- I will be open to true intimacy rather than hide in busy-ness.

My Gratitude:

- I am grateful for the person who has relieved me of so many stressful burdens.
- I am grateful for the many ways I can be of service to others.

Ten of Cups

General Associations

Number: Resolution, completion, results, consolidation, fulfillment.
Suit: Water, emotions, relationships, feeling, heart/soul, human/angel, summer.

Interpretations and Keywords

A happy home, tranquility, contentment, strong affection, attaining happiness, good family relationships.

Example Intentions Using the Intentional Tarot Layout

My Understanding:

The person I'm concerned about

- comes from a happy, stable home.
- always sees the rainbow, finds the best out of any situation.

The situation I'm focused on

- involves my home and family.
- seems to be one of complete joy and happiness.
- represents what others expect of me: marriage and children.

My Goal:

Supplication form:

- Please help my friend find the happiness they deserve.
- Please help me feel complete and content with what I have.

Manifestation form:

- The promise has been fulfilled.
- My family gets along well and loves each other very much.
- I have never been so happy in my life.

My Promise:

- I will look for ways to bring joy into my life.
- I will provide my family with unconditional love.
- I will nurture the relationships I have.

My Gratitude:

- I am grateful for my family.
- I am grateful to be able to experience security and tranquility.

Ten of Swords

General Associations
Number: Resolution, completion, results, consolidation, fulfillment.
Suit: Air, ideas, information, thinking, mind, eagle, autumn.

Interpretations and Keywords
The ultimate attack, betrayal, disaster, final endings, beyond hope, surrendering to misfortune, making the worst of a bad situation, a new dawn on the horizon.

Example Intentions Using the Intentional Tarot Layout

My Understanding:

The person I'm concerned about

- has given up hope.

- might be overreacting to the situation.

- has been the victim of a violent act or malicious gossip.

The situation I'm focused on

- involves a personal disaster.

- is one of the worst times I've ever gone through.

My Goal:

Supplication form:

- Please help us understand what has happened and how things could have turned out so badly.

- Please help my friend see that further efforts will probably end badly for them.

Manifestation form:

- After several unsuccessful applications I have finally gotten a job offer.

My Promise:

- I will try to know when enough is enough.

- I will not act on my revenge fantasies.

My Gratitude:

- I am grateful for the hope on the horizon.

- I am grateful for those who helped me escape from my looping self-deprecating thoughts.

Ten of Pentacles

General Associations

Number: Resolution, completion, results, consolidation, fulfillment.
Suit: Earth, things, money, sensation, body, ox, winter.

Interpretations and Keywords

A prosperous home, joy, abundance, stability, inheritance, tradition, security, excess.

Example Intentions Using the Intentional Tarot Layout

My Understanding:

The person/people I'm concerned about

- are members of my family.
- is a member of a large or well-to-do family.

The situation I'm focused on

- involves a mysterious visitor, stranger, customer, or client.
- involves an inheritance.
- involves a vital community.
- involves great wealth and/or excellent health.

My Goal:

Supplication form:

- Please help my family prosper.
- Please help me be able to remain in my home.

Manifestation form:

- My parents are comfortable in their current living arrangements and are well looked after.
- Our leaders are making laws and rules that support family needs.

My Promise:

- I will honor my family's traditions and values.
- I will clean my house regularly and keep up with repairs.
- I will welcome guests into my home and community.
- I will find ways to live that show respect to the earth.

My Gratitude:

- I am grateful for the home comforts I have.
- I am grateful for the good things I see all around me.
- I am grateful for the struggles of my ancestors.

Page of Wands

General Associations

Rank: New ideas, receptive, optimistic, exploring, vulnerable, inexperienced, student, messenger.

Suit: Fire, will, passion, intuition, soul/spirit, lion, spring.

Interpretations and Keywords

A promising protégé, enjoys being the center of attention, energetic, innovative, enthusiastic, spontaneous, something new to be passionate about.

Example Intentions Using the Intentional Tarot Layout

My Understanding:

The person I'm concerned about

- is enthusiastic about many things in their life.
- is a faithful friend.
- likes to be the center of attention.
- is taking a spontaneous new direction in their life.

The situation I'm focused on

- involves a new product that must be tested before going on the market.
- involves a spur of the moment, fun experience.

My Goal:

Supplication form:

- Please help my friend be decisive when it's time to act on opportunities.
- Please help my child feel validated and appreciated.

Manifestation form:

- The message I've been waiting for has arrived and I'm eager to take the next steps.
- Our group is excited about our new ideas and we are ready to get going.

My Promise:

- I will live in the moment and enjoy this time for now.
- I will think through many options for this situation.
- I will mentor a person who is starting out.

My Gratitude:

- I am grateful for the simple joys in life.
- I am grateful for the fresh energy of our new co-worker.
- I am grateful for the risks I have taken.

Page of Cups

General Associations

Rank: New ideas, receptive, optimistic, exploring, vulnerable, inexperienced, student, messenger.
Suit: Water, emotions, relationships, feeling, heart/soul, human/angel, summer.

Interpretations and Keywords

A loyal friend, enjoys dreams and stories, responsive, comforting, new creative ideas, romantic, sentimental, can be sensitive and full of angst.

Example Intentions Using the Intentional Tarot Layout

My Understanding:

The person I'm concerned about

- is kind, sensitive, and/or vulnerable.
- has been working on their psychic abilities.

The situation I'm focused on

- involves a secret or a surprise.
- involves video games, role playing games, and other "nerdy" fun.

My Goal:

Supplication form:

- Please help my child stay focused on their studies.
- Please help my friend find the romance they've been talking about.

Manifestation form:

- I finally understand something about my partner that I've wondered about.
- The message I've been waiting for has arrived and the news is as I expected.

My Promise:

- I will examine my heart before deciding about this situation.
- I will try something new.
- I will be helpful and loyal.
- I will risk showing my feelings.

My Gratitude:

- I am grateful for having someone so wonderful to love.
- I am grateful that my child is so passionate about their interests.

Page of Swords

General Associations
Rank: New ideas, receptive, optimistic, exploring, vulnerable, inexperienced, student, messenger.
Suit: Air, ideas, information, thinking, mind, eagle, autumn.

Interpretations and Keywords
Enjoys making lists and spreadsheets, a new way of thinking, analyzing, contemplating, easily bored, street smart, truth seeker, book lover.

Example Intentions Using the Intentional Tarot Layout

My Understanding:

The person I'm concerned about

- has been faced with a new way of thinking.
- is good at games and contests.
- is concerned with avoiding conflict.
- has become detached from their studies.

The situation I'm focused on

- involves people gossiping or spying on each other.

My Goal:

Supplication form:

- Please help my child effectively manage their time for all their different pursuits.
- Please help me learn all the details of the new software so I can feel comfortable about the new way of doing things.

Manifestation form:

- The message I've been waiting for has arrived, and the information is helpful.
- During the negotiations, both groups are remaining flexible and adaptable around the solution.
- People have embraced the power of being a voter.

My Promise:

- I will welcome challenges and figure out the right thing to do.
- I will try not to get involved with the conflict between my co-workers.
- I will take time to get used to a new situation before I judge.

My Gratitude:

- I am grateful that my child has a teacher who helps them feel challenged.
- I am grateful for all the interesting activities that fill my week.
- I am grateful for the opportunities that stretch my abilities in new ways.

Page of Pentacles

General Associations

Rank: New ideas, receptive, optimistic, exploring, vulnerable, inexperienced, student, messenger.
Suit: Earth, things, money, sensation, body, ox, winter.

Interpretations and Keywords

A loyal helper, enjoys making and selling crafts, aspiring, learning to use resources, down-to-earth, deliberate.

Example Intentions Using the Intentional Tarot Layout

My Understanding:

The person I'm concerned about

- is a student.
- is quiet, thoughtful, and efficient.
- has new software, art materials, or tools, and is learning how to use them.
- always gets the most potential out of whatever they are given.

The situation I'm focused on

- involves a precious gift.

My Goal:

Supplication form:

- Please help my friend develop realistic goals.
- Please help my child understand all the long-term implications involved with the things they are acquiring.

Manifestation form:

- The message I've been waiting for has arrived and my lost item has been found.
- My students have been studying effectively and are ready for the exam.

My Promise:

- I will remember that my partner needs to study and will not be available to do things with me.
- I will treat my things carefully so they last a long time.
- I will try to be practical in this situation.
- I will try to be realistic about my goals.

My Gratitude:

- I am grateful for the chance to go to school.
- I am grateful for what my students are teaching me.
- I am grateful for my resources of time, energy, focus, money, and health.

Knight of Wands

General Associations

Rank: Active, responsible, on a quest, committed, energetic.
Suit: Fire, will, passion, intuition, soul/spirit, lion, spring.

Interpretations and Keywords

A favorite teacher or author, a fearless leader, daring, outgoing, energetic, warm personality, passionately pursuing a goal or adventure, impulsive, reckless.

Example Intentions Using the Intentional Tarot Layout

My Understanding:

The person I'm concerned about

- is eagerly focused on something specific.

- is certain they are right and is taking over the project.

The situation I'm focused on

- involves intense movement such as an explosion or a tornado.

- involves an adventure or an exciting new activity.

My Goal:

Supplication form:

- Please help my friend find the guidance needed to channel their energies appropriately.

- Please help my child feel comfortable about being around more people.

Manifestation form:

- Our team captain is inspiring, and we are playing the best we ever have.

- Our work load has been reconfigured and we are much more focused on a few important things.

My Promise:

- I will keep working on the situation and not let things get stagnant.

- I will speak up and make sure my contributions are listened to.

- I will renew my energies on things I'm passionate about.

My Gratitude:

- I am grateful for having the energy I need to get things done.

- I am grateful for being able to participate in my favorite sports.

- I am grateful for the true creative focus surfacing in my life.

Knight of Cups

General Associations

Rank: Active, responsible, on a quest, committed, energetic.
Suit: Water, emotions, relationships, feeling, heart/soul, human/angel, summer.

Interpretations and Keywords

A dreamy romantic, artistic, receptive, sensitive, idealistic, honest, loyal, following your heart's desire.

Example Intentions Using the Intentional Tarot Layout

My Understanding:

The person I'm concerned about

- is thinking about committing to a relationship.

- enjoys philosophical discussions.

The situation I'm focused on

- involves a dream or a goal.

- is a romantic event.

My Goal:

Supplication form:

- Please help my friend succeed at what they are passionate about.

- Please help me remember the differences between dreams and fantasies.

Manifestation form:

- I have learned how to love and be a caring partner.

- My partner balances times of going out with friends and times focused on our relationship.

My Promise:

- I will shower my love with affection and try to make them happy.

- I will act with compassion and tenderness in this situation.

- I will be steadfast in working on my art.

- I will follow where my emotions lead me with care and deliberation.

- I will follow my heart's curiosity.

My Gratitude:

- I am grateful to be able to be of help to someone.

- I am grateful for the times of romance in my life.

Knight of Swords

General Associations

Rank: Active, responsible, on a quest, committed, energetic.
Suit: Air, ideas, information, thinking, mind, eagle, autumn.

Interpretations and Keywords

A systems analyst or administrator, highly focused on a plan or goal, direct communicator, evidenced-based ideas, a "knight in shining armor," aggressive, confrontational, heedless of feelings.

Example Intentions Using the Intentional Tarot Layout

My Understanding:

The person I'm concerned about

- is sometimes insensitive to others' feelings.

- is opinionated and sure of themselves.

- is a workaholic.

The situation I'm focused on

- involves important software that is not working, and requires a good programmer to come in and fix it.

- involves something unexpected and sudden; quick decisions must be made.

My Goal:

Supplication form:

- Please help my friend find a career that is interesting and useful.

- Please help me deal effectively with the person who has been confrontational with me.

Manifestation form:

- The new employee or volunteer is a welcome addition to our team and is helping us catch up on our back-load of projects.

- My partner has finished their military deployment and is returning home safely.

My Promise:

- I will do whatever I can to be useful in this situation.

- I will mentor an energetic young person.

- I will try to communicate more clearly.

- I will let go of being a perfectionist.

My Gratitude:

- I am grateful for my friend who is always charging in to my defense.

- I am grateful that my problem was resolved quickly.

Knight of Pentacles

General Associations

Rank: Active, responsible, on a quest, committed, energetic.
Suit: Earth, things, money, sensation, body, ox, winter.

Interpretations and Keywords

Actions that promote financial security, a reliable accountant or investment manager, the security of routines, methodical, cautious, efficient, a realist.

Example Intentions Using the Intentional Tarot Layout

My Understanding:

The person I'm concerned about

- is strong and hard working.
- is a person (or team) that is training for an important event.

The situation I'm focused on

- involves a construction project.
- requires a steady, reliable, thoughtful leader.

My Goal:

Supplication form:

- Please help me have the patience to wait for the right moment to act in this situation.
- Please help my friend get the construction or manufacturing job they want.

Manifestation form:

- The new person at work/church/volunteer organization is being a significant help with practical and useful tasks.
- Our team has been steadfast in chipping away at this large task that needs to get done.

My Promise:

- I will forge ahead on this situation in a steady, calm manner.
- I will consider all factors around this situation.
- I will be a loyal and considerate friend.
- I will wait for clear instructions on what to do.

My Gratitude:

- I am grateful for the strengths I have.
- I am grateful for the help I'm getting on this project.

Queen of Wands

General Associations

Rank: Influential, mentor, supportive, persuasive, inner control.
Suit: Fire, will, passion, intuition, soul/spirit, lion, spring.

Interpretations and Keywords

A performer or public speaker, a passionate supporter, inspirational, a sunny attitude, confident, creative, intuitive, dramatic, love of the home and family.

Example Intentions Using the Intentional Tarot Layout

My Understanding:

The person I'm concerned about

- is energetic, passionate, good natured.
- has been helpful and inspiring.

The situation I'm focused on

- involves my house or apartment.
- involves doing something outside of one's comfort zone.

My Goal:

Supplication form:

- Please help my friend be more confident.
- Please help keep the forest fires away from my house and neighborhood.

Manifestation form:

- My house is sturdy, all the repairs have gone well.
- My pet has recovered from surgery and is healthy.

My Promise:

- I will stop procrastinating and just get started.
- I will put renewed focus on my career.
- I will counsel those who ask for advice.
- I will honor my sensuality.

My Gratitude:

- I am grateful for the strong women in my life.
- I am grateful for my home and pets.
- I am grateful to have creative skills and talents.

Queen of Cups

General Associations

Rank: Influential, mentor, supportive, persuasive, inner control.
Suit: Water, emotions, relationships, feeling, heart/soul, human/angel, summer.

Interpretations and Keywords

A psychologist or a psychic, spiritual, approachable, instinctual, a painter or poet, harmony, tranquility, sensitivity, imagination.

Example Intentions Using the Intentional Tarot Layout

My Understanding:

The person I'm concerned about

- is sensitive, empathetic, and loving.
- is an artist, psychic, therapist, or yoga teacher.
- is raising a child/children.
- has a lot of friends and many people cherish their friendship.

The situation I'm focused on

- involves a project that is progressing smoothly.

My Goal:

Supplication form:

- Please help my friend direct their imagination into something that can be actualized.
- Please help me find an objective listener to help me understand my relationship problems.

Manifestation form:

- My mother is taking a well-deserved rest from her generous care of others.
- We have found a patron to support our creative efforts.

My Promise:

- I will act in this situation with love, looking to the needs of others.
- I will focus my art with directed creative energies.
- I will nurture my romantic relationship.
- I will take time to meditate regularly.

My Gratitude:

- I am grateful that I can pour my heart out to my friends.
- I am grateful for my creative impulses and abilities.

Queen of Swords

General Associations

Rank: Influential, mentor, supportive, persuasive, inner control.
Suit: Air, ideas, information, thinking, mind, eagle, autumn.

Interpretations and Keywords

An effective project manager, a good communicator, highly intelligent, unemotional, efficient, brutally honest, impartial.

Example Intentions Using the Intentional Tarot Layout

My Understanding:

The person I'm concerned about

- is an intelligent person who has had many intense experiences in their life.
- is someone known for "kicking butt and taking names."
- is a strong-willed matriarch, "an iron fist in a velvet glove."

The situation I'm focused on

- involves a new manager with many plans that will affect my workplace.
- involves the passing of someone's spouse.

My Goal:

Supplication form:

- Please help my child continue to learn how to be independent.
- Please help me cut through the red tape and just get things done.

Manifestation form:

- The new manager at the civil agency I have to deal with is effectively straightening out their disorganized situation.
- The journalist has received awards for their reporting of the facts.

My Promise:

- I will listen to the advice I'm given, even if it seems harsh.
- I will let my head rule my heart in this situation.
- I will contribute what I can to the plans being made.

My Gratitude:

- I am grateful for someone who can be honest with me.
- I am grateful that I can live an independent life.
- I am grateful for my experiences, both good and bad.

Queen of Pentacles

General Associations

Rank: Influential, mentor, supportive, persuasive, inner control.

Suit: Earth, things, money, sensation, body, ox, winter.

Interpretations and Keywords

A patron of the arts or event coordinator, practical, resourceful, care for the physical environment, the love of beautiful things.

Example Intentions Using the Intentional Tarot Layout

My Understanding:

The person I'm concerned about

- loves being in nature.
- works at helping others reach their best potential.
- is responsible and financially secure.
- is creative and practical.

The situation I'm focused on

- involves a store or a restaurant.
- involves leadership with feminine energy.

My Goal:

Supplication form:

- Please help us sell our house.
- Please help my friend with her efforts to get pregnant.
- Please help my friend get the job they applied for.

Manifestation form:

- My friend has found their confidence and knows that life is good.
- Our organization is dependable and useful to the people who rely on what we provide.
- I have the resources I need and am financially comfortable.

My Promise:

- I will make the effort to spend more time outdoors.
- I will visualize achieving my goals.
- I will make the most of an unpleasant situation.
- I will help my friend plan their big event.

My Gratitude:

- I am grateful for our public open spaces.
- I am grateful for the abundance of the marketplace and the options we have to buy things.
- I am grateful for getting my home to look just the way I want.

King of Wands

General Associations

Rank: Authority, success, experience, decisiveness, external control.
Suit: Fire, will, passion, intuition, soul/spirit, lion, spring.

Interpretations and Keywords

A charismatic leader, strong willed, charming, enterprising, passionate, inspires creativity.

Example Intentions Using the Intentional Tarot Layout

My Understanding:

The person I'm concerned about

- is a business person, entrepreneur, or politician.
- is strong minded, always thinks they're right.
- loves being in nature.

The situation I'm focused on

- involves a political campaign.
- involves someone who needs a spark of inspiration.

My Goal:

Supplication form:

- Please help us influence the investors with our passion for our project.
- Please help my friend learn how to control their energies.

Manifestation form:

- The job interview went well and the interviewers were impressed with my passion for the work.
- The votes are all in and our candidate has won the election.

My Promise:

- I will actively support this person's political campaign.
- I will try to keep my energy flowing in this situation.
- I will mentor someone who needs encouragement.

My Gratitude:

- I am grateful for the services this person has provided to the community.
- I am grateful for the passion my team is putting toward the project.

King of Cups

General Associations

Rank: Authority, success, experience, decisiveness, external control.
Suit: Water, emotions, relationships, feeling, heart/soul, human/angel, summer.

Interpretations and Keywords

Protective, affectionate, diplomatic, spiritual, a counselor, a medical or artistic professional, empathy, sincerity.

Example Intentions Using the Intentional Tarot Layout

My Understanding:

The person I'm concerned about

- is a doctor, counselor, or patron of the arts.

- is a confident sensitive person in touch with their feelings.

- can be persuaded by a good sob story.

The situation I'm focused on

- involves an organization that tries to do the right thing, treats their clients/customers with respect and dignity.

My Goal:

Supplication form:

- Please help my friend stay connected to their creative side.

- Please help me find the right doctor for my condition.

Manifestation form:

- Our new manager at work is sincere and emotionally well balanced.

- The news media is reporting the true impact of the situation's effects on people, and the public is becoming engaged in the issue.

My Promise:

- I will learn to be more expressive with my emotions.

- I will keep my passions under control.

- I will try to be a wise listener.

My Gratitude:

- I am grateful for the excellent medical care available to me.

- I am grateful for the moral courage of some of our leaders.

King of Swords

General Associations

Rank: Authority, success, experience, decisiveness, external control.
Suit: Air, ideas, information, thinking, mind, eagle, autumn.

Interpretations and Keywords

Makes decisions based on reasoning and logic, truthful, witty, decisive, calculating, a scientist, analyst, or lawyer.

Example Intentions Using the Intentional Tarot Layout

My Understanding:

The person I'm concerned about

- is an authority with a sharp mind.
- can be cold and aloof sometimes.
- has been through a lot and has learned life's lessons.

The situation I'm focused on

- involves uncovering facts and making decisions.
- involves acting on one's principles.

My Goal:

Supplication form:

- Please help my friend recognize the truth about this situation.
- Please help law enforcement officials keep everyone safe.

Manifestation form:

- My surgeon is highly skilled, and the operation has been a success.
- The investigator has uncovered all the facts they need to make a valid case.

My Promise:

- I will prepare for talking with this person by getting all my facts straight.
- I will take a step back from this situation and look at the whole picture.
- I will talk to my parent about treating people with gentleness.

My Gratitude:

- I am grateful for community leaders who understand society's problems and are acting to correct them.
- I am grateful that my organization is strong enough to advocate for what is right.
- I am grateful for those who have shown me how to effectively hold my own power.

King of Pentacles

General Associations

Rank: Authority, success, experience, decisiveness, external control.
Suit: Earth, things, money, sensation, body, ox, winter.

Interpretations and Keywords

Focused on the bottom line, a business leader or collector, generous, practical, stable, traditional, love of the earth.

Example Intentions Using the Intentional Tarot Layout

My Understanding:

The person I'm concerned about

- is a realtor, engineer, or business professional.
- loves the outdoors.
- is generous and has a lot to give.
- is skeptical of the esoteric arts.

The situation I'm focused on

- requires hard work and perseverance.
- involves a home security company or system or a hacking situation.

My Goal:

Supplication form:

- Please help my friend appreciate and enjoy their accomplishments.
- Please help us see all the potential possibilities in the opportunity before us.

Manifestation form:

- My organization is in a good financial position and the employees, volunteers, or members are feeling well rewarded.
- The patriarch is learning to treat their family gently and to respect everyone's opinions.

My Promise:

- I will acknowledge the privileges I have.
- I will make the best out of whatever resources are available.
- I will commit to managing what resources I have in a vital way.

My Gratitude:

- I am grateful for the good things I have.
- I am grateful for the reliability of my friends.

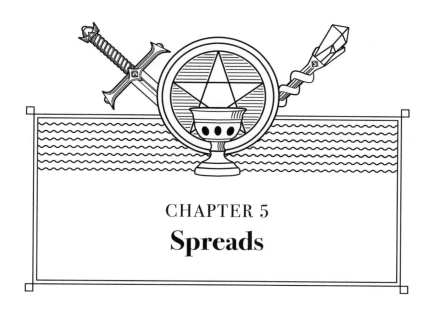

CHAPTER 5
Spreads

Spreads for Traditional Readings

Past Present Future

This spread can give you a quick look at your issue from a time-centered perspective.

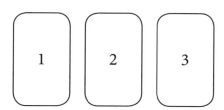

1. The recent past
2. The present moment
3. The near future

> *To activate this spread: After completing your interpretation,*
> *look through the cards face-up and select one or two that*

represent the future you would like to see. Picture energy flowing like a wheel from the universe, through the cards you were given and the cards showing your desires, then back to the universe with gratitude and hope.

Two Paths

If you have a choice to make, this spread can illuminate different aspects of each possibility.

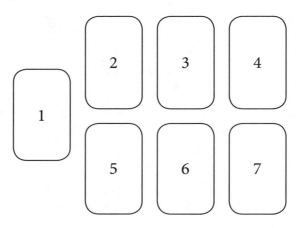

1. You, at the crossroads

2, 3, and 4. Path A, benefits, downsides, and probable outcome

5, 6, and 7. Path B, benefits, downsides, and probable outcome.

> *To activate this spread: After completing your interpretation, look through the cards face-up.*
>
> - *If you are drawn to one of the paths, place cards on that path that symbolize how you would wish it to unfold.*
> - *If you are drawn to neither path or both paths, place cards in line with the first card that express your longer-term desires, perhaps 10 or 20 years past this decision point.*

Picture energy flowing like a wheel from the universe, through the cards you were given and the cards showing your desires, then back to the universe with gratitude and hope.

The Fool's Journey

This is a "what do I need to know right now?" type of spread. The four corners represent the four aspects of your metaphysical being (body, mind, heart, and soul), and the center row represents your own Fool's Journey. The cards that appear indicate an important aspect of each area.

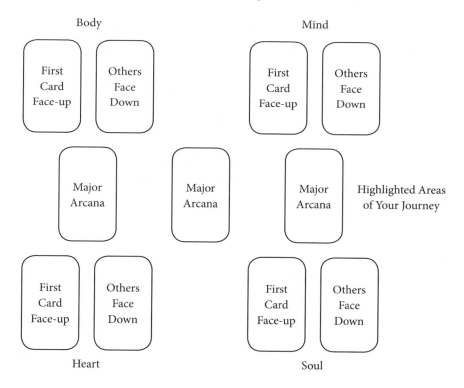

Placing the cards:

1. Shuffle and cut the cards and draw from the top of the deck.
2. Place Major Arcana cards on The Fool's Journey row. Place Minor Arcana cards in their proper corner: Pentacles = Body, Swords = Mind, Cups = Heart, Wands = Soul.

3. If you get more suit cards for an area that already has a face-up card, place it face down in that corner. You will count these to see how important this life aspect is right now.

4. Keep drawing and placing cards until there is one face-up card in each of the four corners.

Reading the cards:

1. The face-up cards in the Body, Mind, Heart, and Soul corners reflect specific aspects of those parts of your life that are important right now. The number of face-down cards indicates the current relative importance of that area.

2. The cards in The Fool's Journey row highlight those stages of the Journey that you should be giving special consideration to right now.

> *To activate this spread: After completing your interpretation, decide which corner of the spread is of most concern to you right now. Look through the cards face up and select cards that express your desires for that aspect of your life. Picture energy flowing like a wheel from the universe, through the cards you were given and the cards showing your desires, then back to the universe with gratitude and hope.*

Celtic Cross

This is the spread I normally use, even for my own readings. With ten cards, the reading is not too long or too short and the positions cover a nicely comprehensive look at the issue being brought forth. The first tarot book I studied had position meanings like "this covers you" and "this crowns you" which didn't mean much to me, so I tweaked the wording of the positions for my own use. And, as with anything in the tarot, my understanding and use of this tool keeps evolving. Sometimes just one reading with a person will illuminate a new aspect of a card or a position and this new understanding will stick with me and influence how I see things going forward. This is why my wording for the positions might be different from others you may find.

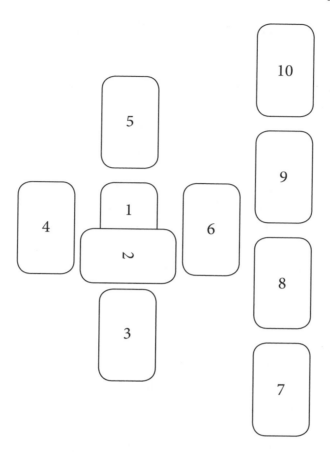

The text in quotes is what I say out loud as I lay down the card; the other text is how I use this card in the reading.

1. "This is the situation." Sometimes the querent can see themselves in this card; other times this illustrates the core of the issue, such as a crabby boss.

2. "This is the energy of the situation." This can be either a positive or negative energy working in the issue.

3. "This is the foundation of the situation." This is the background of the issue or some factors related to how it came about.

4. "This is the recent past." I consider this to relate to things that happened in the past month or so.

5. "This is a major influence on the situation." I tell the querent that this could be a strong external influence or the influence they are having if they are already working toward their goals in the situation. I usually talk with the querent about what is happening between the Major Influence card and the Energy of the Situation card.

6. "This is the near future." (I don't put down the Future card right after the Past card because I like to go in a circle.) I consider this to be a glimpse into the next few weeks.

7. "This is how you see yourself in this situation." It's statistically improbable the number of times I've seen the Knight of Swords (knight in shining armor) and the Ten of Wands (overburdened person) in this position. Yet that's how the tarot works sometimes.

8. "This is how others see you in this situation." This is sometimes the most revealing aspect of the spread and often the one my friends look forward to the most.

9. "This is your hopes and fears for the situation." Sometimes this is the most complex card to interpret in the reading.

10. "This is the most likely outcome if things keep going on as they are." I always talk to the querent about how the Major Influences card could bring about changes to this potential outcome.

> *To activate this spread: After completing your interpretation, examine the "Most Likely Outcome" card. Look through the cards face-up and select cards that express the outcome you truly wish to see. These cards can enhance the card that the universe has sent or can indicate a desire for something different to manifest. You can take cards from the spread or select from a second deck if you want to use those cards but prefer to keep the spread intact. Picture energy flowing like a wheel from the universe, through the cards you were given and the cards showing your desires, then back to the universe with gratitude and hope.*

Spreads for Intentional Tarot
The Yes Path, the No Path, and the Make-It-So Path

One of my favorite traditional layouts is the *Two Paths* spread. Readings using this spread often help me see my options and make me think of what could happen depending on the actions I take to pursue one path or the other. In the proactive spirit of Intentional Tarot, you approach the three spreads below from the perspective of already having made your choice and knowing if you want things to change, to be protected from change, or to manifest something new. I find these spreads to be easier to do with non-RWS-type decks. Since the images on those cards can depict literally anything, I find it easier to let my subconscious take over and project what I'm thinking about into a single card.

The Yes Path: Use this spread when you are ready to embrace *change*.

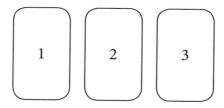

1. Describe the situation you want to change.

2. Describe the change that would be of benefit in this situation.

3. Use this card to focus on the situation evolving from its current state to your preferred state.

The No Path: Use this spread for *protection* of either a person or a situation.

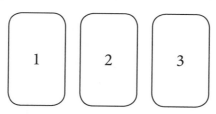

1. Describe the person, place, or situation you want to protect.

2. Describe the negative consequences that might happen if a threatened change occurs, including accidental or systemic.

3. Use this card to focus on the person or situation being safe from negative influences.

The Make-It-So Path: Use this spread when you want to *manifest* something new or wonderful in your life.

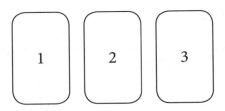

1. Describe the outcome that you want to manifest.

2. Describe the benefit to those concerned if this outcome came to pass.

3. Use this card to focus on your desired outcome as if it has already occurred and is active in your life right now.

The Intentional Tarot Spread

The Intentional Tarot spread is described in chapter 3. When I think through the four concepts in this spread, I feel like the energy I'm sending to the universe is a complete package, wherein all bases are covered around the situation. While the illustration below shows only one card in each position, I usually need three or four cards in some positions to fully embody my understanding of the situation and my goals. I try not to go over four cards in any one position.

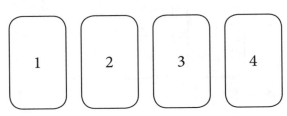

Position Meanings

1. My Understanding: Describe how you understand the situation that you want to affect.

2. My Goal: This is the outcome you think would be of benefit to those involved. It could be just general good wishes and positive energy, leaving it up to the universe to work things out for the best.

3. My Promise: Beyond thoughts and prayers, think of an action you can do to help bring about your goal.

4. My Gratitude: Describe something related to the situation that you are grateful for.

Some people will see a strong connection between the energies we send out in Intentional Tarot and the prayer traditions they practice. The following series of spreads might be interesting to Precants who find meaning and comfort in different prayer traditions.

Om/AUM

In the Hindu tradition, the sound of om (or AUM), is considered to represent the oneness of all things. When chanted correctly, the sound of all possible words is present in AUM. This spread can be used with Intentional Tarot for the goal of eventual enlightenment of all sentient beings.

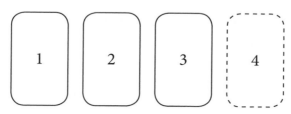

1. A, Advent: The beginning of your wish for enlightenment for all.

2. U, Upsight: A deeper understanding of what it means to be enlightened.

3. M, Manifestation: Your sense of how things would feel when all are enlightened.

4. Silence: This position is left empty to represent the silence after the sound AUM.

Prayer Flags

Tibetan prayer flags do not represent the classic concept of prayer. Instead their very flag-ness and elevated physical presence let them be something spiritually unique. It's not the flags themselves but the wind that flows through them that is blessed. This blessing extends to all people and things touched by the wind. This spread might require a stronger familiarity with the relationships between different cards.

- Decide on a blessing you would like to extend to your community.
- Select a card for each position, ideally in the suit indicated below if it fits with your blessing.
- Consider the relationships between all the cards you are selecting, not just the cards that are positioned next to each other.
- Focus on these relationships among all the cards as you send out energy to the universe, and not on the individual card intentions.

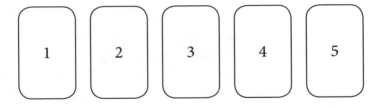

1. Blue/Space/major arcana: The main thought of your blessing.
2. White/Air/Swords: The logical aspect of your blessing.
3. Red/Fire/Wands: The thing that inspires you to present this blessing.
4. Green/Water/Cups: How you feel about this blessing.
5. Yellow/Earth/Pentacles: A physical aspect about this blessing.

The Cathedral

In medieval times entering a church would give one sanctuary from those who pursued them. This spread would be a good tool to use when using Intentional Tarot for the protection of a specific person.

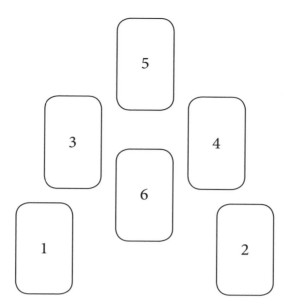

1 and 2, The Foundation: Describe the basics of the situation and how it started.

3 and 4, The Windows: Describe the subtleties that color the situation and your goals for protecting this person.

5, The Icon: This represents your Deity or the universe or the essence of whatever it is you are sending your energies out to. Contemplate the properties of and your relationship to this entity.

6, The Person: This person is the focus of your energies; picture them sheltered and safe from harm.

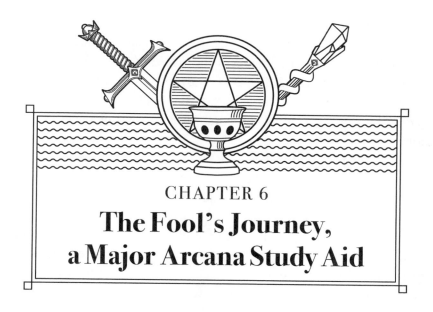

CHAPTER 6
The Fool's Journey, a Major Arcana Study Aid

One element that makes a tarot deck unique among divinatory tools is its two-part nature, the major arcana and the minor arcana. When you do a reading with all seventy-eight cards, you are interweaving two distinct perspectives of life, both the day-to-day "outer world" events common to most people (friendship, heartbreak, memories, generosity, confusion, etc.) and the deeper "inner world" stages that many people approach and deal with repeatedly in their lives, such as understanding our core strengths or admitting our harmful habits and tendencies. This journey of internal development represented by the major arcana can be experienced at a small scale in separate facets of our lives (such as the beginning, middle, and possible end of a relationship), as well as at the all-encompassing scale of our ideal life-long journey to self-actualization, or the realization our full potential.

The individual twenty-two cards of the major arcana are rich in their unique meanings and symbolism and can be studied as stand-alone aspects of the human condition. Insightful patterns can be found in the relationships between cards that are adjacent or far apart, without bringing in the aspect of progressing through a journey from the lower numbered cards to the higher numbered. For example, Justice can be seen as a balancing or fairness aspect between the "stuff happens" feeling of the Wheel of Fortune and the loss of control feeling of the Hanged Man. The joyful feeling of the Lovers card is often mirrored in the dreadful aspect of the Devil card. Many tarot books describe the cards, excluding the Fool, in three rows of seven cards, and ascribe a significant life theme to each row. The Fool's Journey is by no means the only or the preferred pattern to look for in the major arcana. However, this chapter will focus on The Fool's Journey from the perspective of studying the tarot as a beginner and as an aid for remembering the classic names of all twenty-two cards and the order in which they appear in the tarot.

As described in chapter 1, for this study aid I'm presenting the major arcana in twenty-two stages of five cards, each stage progressing one card further down The Fool's Journey. This allows us to see all the adjacent relationships and focus on each card in its turn. The tool begins with the Fool, which seems proper. This puts the High Priestess in the happy position as our first focus, which also seems proper since the Fool presumably begins their journey as a quest for understanding the secrets of divine wisdom. Thus, in this arrangement, the tool ends with the Magician in the center focus position. Finding the Magician so near the end of our studies, with High Priestess and the Empress appearing again at the end, helps underscore that our Journey continues through many cycles. We can be on different parts of the archetypal journey within different parts of our lives simultaneously.

Along the journey, the Fool confronts many archetypal situations, either depicted by one or more people in the scene or by iconic images such as the Wheel of Fortune and the Tower. This tool presents the Fool as dealing with the concepts of the cards from both an external perspective, where they "meet" the character or are affected by the icon, and from an internal perspective, where they "are" the character or are producing the action of the icon. The latter is important to remember when the cards show up in positions such as "This is you in this situation" or "This is how you see yourself in this situation."

I'm happy that the pronouns "they" and "their" are becoming standard for referring to a person of any or unknown gender. I think this lets students of any gender feel more connected to the Fool and their journey. Remember that this is just one tool for remembering the major arcana, and the phrases presented below are not intended as fully complete meanings for each of the cards.

The Fool's Journey Major Arcana Study Aid

As stated in the *Getting Off Book* section in chapter 1, the purpose of each five-card stage is to help you become familiar with the major arcana cards and the order in which they appear. In chapter 1 are suggested steps for practicing with The Fool's Journey study aid grid. To summarize:

- Place a stage's five cards before you.
- Develop a story of what the Fool might be experiencing in this portion of their journey.
- Read about the five cards in your tarot reference books.
- Pay particular attention to the center card in the stage.
- When trying to get off book, study only one stage per day.

Space has been provided for you to note your own feelings and impressions of each stage in the journey. You may wish to write out a story from your life when you experienced one or more of the stages illustrated. Or you could create a short story complete with descriptive scenes and dialog between the characters. As you work with the journey in different ways, the themes of major arcana will have more and more meaning to you.

Stage 1
0–Fool, 1–Magician, 2–High Priestess,
3–Empress, 4–Emperor

The Fool's Progress: The Fool begins their journey in innocence. They are only lightly burdened and are not alone. They have the tools they need for the journey, even if they are in a very raw state. They yearn to know the mysteries of life, beyond what they have been taught by their parents.

The Fool meets the High Priestess: She initiates the Fool into the beginning of the journey.

The Fool as the High Priestess: The Fool must stay calm and call on their intuition to learn the secrets of what is in the scroll and beyond the veil.

Additional Notes: _____

_____

_____

_____

_____

_____

_____

_____

_____

_____

_____

_____

Stage 2
1–Magician, 2–High Priestess, 3–Empress, 4–Emperor, 5–Hierophant

The Fool's Progress: With their tools and their goal in mind, the Fool bids good-bye to their parents and begins their formal education.

The Fool meets the Empress: She is the Mother figure, warm and loving.

The Fool as the Empress: The Fool understands their softer side. They feel a willingness to provide love and support for others along the way.

Additional Notes: _____

_____

_____

_____

_____

_____

_____

_____

_____

_____

_____

_____

_____

_____

_____

Stage 3
2–High Priestess, 3–Empress, 4–Emperor,
5–Hierophant, 6–Lovers

The Fool's Progress: The first issue the Fool deals with in their self-discovery relates to their sexuality and gender. The feminine energies and the masculine energies ideally lead the Fool to finding the appropriate balance that works for them. They explore romantic and sexual relationships.

The Fool meets the Emperor: He is the Father figure, stable and secure, perhaps judgmental.

The Fool as the Emperor: The Fool understands firmness and confidence. They know they can make decisions on their journey and expect people to respect those decisions.

Additional Notes: _____

_____

_____

_____

_____

_____

_____

_____

_____

_____

_____

Stage 4
3–Empress, 4–Emperor, 5–Hierophant, 6–Lovers, 7–Chariot

The Fool's Progress: A complicated and frustrating phase; parents, teachers, and lovers all looking for attention. The Fool might want to escape it all.

The Fool meets the Hierophant: He is the perceived authority, in many ways the opposite of the High Priestess. While she encourages you to begin your journey, he is already testing you to see if you should continue.

The Fool as the Hierophant: The Fool understands they need to stay true to their beliefs. They know where they are going and that not just any road can take them there.

Additional Notes: _____

_____

_____

_____

_____

_____

_____

_____

_____

_____

_____

_____

_____

Stage 5
4–Emperor, 5–Hierophant, 6–Lovers,
7–Chariot, 8–Strength

The Fool's Progress: The Fool pulls away from the most demanding parts of their previous existence and learns how to face the new challenges ahead of them.

The Fool meets the angel Raphael and the two Lovers: It seems that everyone is in a relationship and that most popular songs and movies are about love going wrong or being the culmination of a story.

The Fool as a Lover: The Fool understands that external influences make a relationship complicated. Parents, friends, gossip, social media, everyone observing them. All must be dealt with when inside a relationship. (In the Two of Cups card, the Fool enjoys the bliss of being loved and having a beloved.)

Additional Notes: _____

_____

_____

_____

_____

_____

_____

_____

_____

Stage 6
5–Hierophant, 6–Lovers, 7–Chariot,
8–Strength, 9–Hermit

The Fool's Progress: Still in the early stages of the Journey, the Fool feels there is so much to learn, so many distractions; sometimes they want to leave it all behind, but they aren't sure they have the strength to do it. They would appreciate some guidance.

The Fool meets the Charioteer: This person seems like they have everything under control, in an external sense. Everything that the Fool struggles with comes easily to the Charioteer and they have the perfect means to move ahead.

The Fool as the Charioteer: The Fool sometimes feels like they are in a block of cement and that people who might help them are just sleeping on the job. It takes an enormous effort of will to get things moving in a specific direction and actually make progress.

Additional Notes: _____

_____

_____

_____

_____

_____

_____

_____

_____

Stage 7
6–Lovers, 7–Chariot, 8–Strength,
9–Hermit, 10–Wheel of Fortune

The Fool's Progress: With a better understanding of how to handle different relationships, the Fool moves on, learning about their own strengths and wisdom. They are ready for whatever lies ahead.

The Fool meets Strength and her lion: Like the Chariot, here is a second person who seems in control of their life, but in an internal sense; she remains calm even when facing her own personal demons.

The Fool as Strength dealing with the lion: The Fool understands that they should not be stressed out by possible challenges and dangers. They can be calm and confident even when emotional situations threaten to tear them apart.

Additional Notes: _____

_____

_____

_____

_____

_____

_____

_____

_____

_____

Stage 8
7–Chariot, 8–Strength, 9–Hermit,
10–Wheel of Fortune, 11–Justice

The Fool's Progress: The Fool is moving in full flow. Like a person in the prime of life, they just "get it." They've gained strength and wisdom, the fates flow around them, and all seems balanced.

The Fool meets the Hermit: Watching the Fool's progress from on high, the Hermit uses their lamp to draw the Fool into the elder's path so they can provide needed guidance.

The Fool as the Hermit: The Fool understands that they need and want to spend time alone for introspection and to think through plans and ideas.

Additional Notes: _____

_____

_____

_____

_____

_____

_____

_____

_____

_____

_____

_____

Stage 9
8–Strength, 9–Hermit, 10–Wheel of Fortune, 11–Justice, 12–Hanged Man

The Fool's Progress: Things continue smoothly for the Fool but at a deeper level. At the pinnacle of life, as the fates continue to bless them with strength and wisdom, they begin to see the need to pause and give back to the community. They start to see the world from new perspectives.

The Fool is tied to the Wheel of Fortune: What goes up must come down and the Fool's fortunes begin to change as the Wheel turns. Some change is gradual, and some will suddenly turn their world upside down.

The Fool spins the Wheel of Fortune: The Fool understands that their actions can affect others. Whether they sacrifice something to help someone out or they select among applicants for a job posting, they know they can make the Wheel spin in others' lives.

Additional Notes: _____

_____

_____

_____

_____

_____

_____

_____

_____

_____

Stage 10
9–Hermit, 10–Wheel of Fortune, 11–Justice, 12–Hanged Man, 13–Death

The Fool's Progress: The Fool has the wisdom to see that perhaps the fates have shifted a bit for them. They try to remain calm as changes in relationships, jobs, or world events inevitably occur. They are wise enough to know that nothing lasts forever.

The Fool meets Justice: She is the impartial judge with eyes open to see that truth gets served.

The Fool as Justice: The Fool understands that to provide justice they need to be balanced and patient. They have assumed a new level of responsibility.

Additional Notes: _____

_____

_____

_____

_____

_____

_____

_____

_____

_____

_____

_____

Stage 11
10–Wheel of Fortune, 11–Justice, 12–Hanged Man, 13–Death, 14–Temperance

The Fool's Progress: The Wheel turns and, in order to keep things balanced, all is turned upside-down. Things come to an end and the Fool faces that fact with patience and poise.

The Fool meets the Hanged Man: He embodies the calm before the storm, the suspension of the moment before life changes to something new.

The Fool as the Hanged Man: The Fool understands that sometimes we can feel powerless as events unfold around us.

Additional Notes: _____

_____

_____

_____

_____

_____

_____

_____

_____

_____

_____

_____

Stage 12
11–Justice, 12–Hanged Man, 13–Death, 14–Temperance, 15–Devil

The Fool's Progress: The Fool is being judged. Their sacrifices and willingness to let go of things are being blended with their bad habits and avaricious behaviors.

The Fool meets Death: This is the sense of grief for what has been lost. While it allows for movement to the next thing, there is still sadness and loss.

The Fool as Death: The Fool understands that by leaving a home, a relationship, or a job, they can be an agent of unwanted change for others.

Additional Notes: _____

_____

_____

_____

_____

_____

_____

_____

_____

_____

_____

_____

_____

Stage 13
12–Hanged Man, 13–Death,
14–Temperance, 15–Devil, 16–Tower

The Fool's Progress: The Fool is hanging from a thread. Everything seems lost and they just can't catch a break. Their saving grace is if they can maintain a calm center and manage to bring some equilibrium into their life.

The Fool meets Temperance: This angel is showing the Fool that life consists of a mixture of both good times and bad, success and failure, progress and stalemate.

The Fool as Temperance: The Fool understands that even in the midst of the worst that life can bring, they need to stay calm and let the flow of their actions bring things back into balance.

Additional Notes: _____

_____

_____

_____

_____

_____

_____

_____

_____

_____

_____

Stage 14
13–Death, 14–Temperance,
15–Devil, 16–Tower, 17–Star

The Fool's Progress: In the worst of circumstances, still some hope appears. One cannot move upward until after they have reached their lowest point, but there is always something on the horizon.

The Fool meets the Devil and the two Slaves: The external world can seem full of corruption, people with strange ideas, internet trolls, all manner of dark and depraved stories.

The Fool as a Slave: The Fool understands that some of the things they indulge in are not beneficial to themselves or the people around them.

Additional Notes: _____

_____

_____

_____

_____

_____

_____

_____

_____

_____

_____

_____

_____

Stage 15
14–Temperance, 15–Devil,
16–Tower, 17–Star, 18–Moon

The Fool's Progress: In blending their old life with the new, the Fool realizes that there are foundational differences. Their new life can seem like a mere reflection of how things used to be, but this perception is often due to a distorted memory of our past.

The Fool is within the Tower as it falls: This is a real or metaphorical event that changes everything for the Fool, perhaps a sudden accident or epiphany or an unexpected "we need to have a talk" conversation.

The Fool causes the Tower to fall: The Fool might feel it necessary to let someone know "we need to have a talk." Or perhaps, in order to escape their slavery to the Devil, they need to crush the foundations of where they are imprisoned in order to stop the practice or situation that is keeping them prisoner.

Additional Notes: _____

_____

_____

_____

_____

_____

_____

_____

_____

Stage 16
15–Devil, 16–Tower,
17–Star, 18–Moon, 19–Sun

The Fool's Progress: After looking into their darker side and making some structural changes to how they live in the world, the Fool moves on. The relief of having passed through what has gone before feels as if they are on a higher plane of existence, up among the heavenly bodies. Life becomes warm and good again.

The Fool meets the woman of Star: She might be the naked High Priestess, all her secrets revealed and the divine wisdom that the Fool was seeking at the outset of their Journey is no longer hidden but is shining brightly in the sky where everyone can see.

The Fool as the woman of the Star: The Fool understands that in order to be cleansed and refreshed from what has gone before, they must strip off their previous ideas and bathe in the waters of renewed purpose.

Additional Notes: _____

_____

_____

_____

_____

_____

_____

_____

Stage 17
16–Tower, 17–Star, 18–Moon, 19–Sun, 20–Judgement

The Fool's Progress: Once again, fundamental changes are occurring, but instead of things falling down, things are rising up. Through the steps of cleansing and confusion to clarity, the Fool is truly ready to begin again.

The Fool meets the Moon: The Moon brings a sense of confusion to this part of the Journey. It can be frightening to move on to a new and uncertain period in our lives.

The Fool as the Moon: The Fool understands that things are not always what they seem and that, sometimes, keeping secrets is important.

Additional Notes: _____

_____

_____

_____

_____

_____

_____

_____

_____

_____

_____

_____

Stage 18
17–Star, 18–Moon, 19–Sun, 20–Judgement, 21–World

The Fool's Progress: The Fool transitions from the heavens down to the world again. They have answered the call and find themselves rewarded and fulfilled.

The Fool meets the Sun: The Sun brings joy and brightness to the Fool's path, the feeling that all is right with the world.

The Fool as the Sun: The Fool understands confidence and that they deserve their successes.

Additional Notes: _____

_____

_____

_____

_____

_____

_____

_____

_____

_____

_____

_____

_____

Stage 19
18–Moon, 19–Sun, 20–Judgement,
21–World, 0–Fool

The Fool's Progress: The Fool sees a confusing reflection of themselves. Amidst the joy and satisfaction of their journey's end, a new self arises. The Fool looks back on what has gone before and takes another step forward.

The Fool meets the angel Gabriel sounding the call of Judgement Day: The angel calls to the Fool but the requested action and the Fool's response could be many things. In responding to the call, the Fool faces more changes, but these changes bring new opportunities.

The Fool sends out the call of Judgement Day: At this stage of their journey, the Fool understands they have an option or perhaps an obligation to help others awaken from their confinement of lifeless stasis.

Additional Notes: _____

_____

_____

_____

_____

_____

_____

_____

_____

_____

_____

Stage 20
19–Sun, 20–Judgement,
21–World, 0–Fool, 1–Magician

The Fool's Progress: The Fool has almost come full circle. They feel like a child again who can wave their arms around in joyous abandon as they dance. Soon they gather their wits again and bring all those heavenly energies back down to earth.

The Fool meets the Dancing World: The Dancer brings recognition of the accomplishments of The Fool's Journey and offers rewarding fulfillment.

The Fool as the Dancing World: The Fool understands that they have surpassed many challenges and are now at a new beginning.

Additional Notes: _____

_____

_____

_____

_____

_____

_____

_____

_____

_____

_____

_____

_____

Stage 21
20–Judgement, 21–World, 0–Fool, 1–Magician, 2–High Priestess

The Fool's Progress: The Fool has been reborn. With the gifts of their new understanding they have learned new ways to use the tools they are given in life. They are ready to continue to learn about more of life's mysteries.

The Fool as their new incarnation: The Fool has grown through their experiences yet still retains their innocence. The sun shines brightly on the beginning of a new adventure.

Additional Notes: _____

_____

_____

_____

_____

_____

_____

_____

_____

_____

_____

_____

_____

_____

Stage 22
21–World, 0–Fool, 1–Magician,
2–High Priestess, 3–Empress

The Fool's Progress: As a new journey begins, the Fool still knows the feeling of past accomplishments. Ahead are more mysteries and a life full of rich experiences. This point is the moment of stillness between breaths.

The Fool meets the Magician: He is ready to teach the Fool more about the tools that will be useful as they continue forward.

The Fool as the Magician: All possibilities exist for the Fool as they continue their journey. They draw down the energies of the universe, ground themselves to the earth, and begin again.

Additional Notes: _____

_____

_____

_____

_____

_____

_____

_____

_____

_____

_____

_____

APPENDIX
Card Theme Words

Most tarot books don't need an index or concordance for the cards themselves. When using tarot cards in the traditional manner, the reader selects a spread and lays out the number of cards required. Usually, this is between one and ten (or so) cards. If the reader is not yet off book, they only have that many cards to look up, using whatever card order was chosen for their reference book. An index of card meanings isn't necessary in this situation.

In contrast, when using the cards for an Intentional Tarot spread, the precant has all seventy-eight cards to select from. This can be overwhelming, both for people who are completely new to the tarot as well as for anyone not yet entirely off book. As covered in chapter 3, it's completely appropriate to select cards for an Intentional Tarot spread entirely by letting the images speak to you. However, many people will wish to select cards based on their classic meanings. That's when this list of theme words can be useful.

The theme words in the following list are the keywords for the cards found in chapter 4. No two tarot authors will use the exact same set of words for all the cards, and the words on this list are merely my personal preferences. The margins give you plenty of room to make your own notes. I hope you find them useful when selecting cards for your spreads.

abundance	Ace of Pentacles
abundance	Nine of Pentacles
abundance	Ten of Pentacles
abundance	The Empress
accomplishments	Six of Wands
accountant	Knight of Pentacles
achievements	Six of Wands
act, the time to	Eight of Wands
action	Knight of Pentacles
adaptable	Two of Pentacles
administrator	Knight of Swords
adventure	Knight of Wands
adversity	Six of Swords
advice	The Hermit
affection	Ten of Cups
agendas	Five of Wands
aggressive	Knight of Swords
alone	Three of Swords
ambition	Ace of Wands
analyst	King of Swords
analyzing	Page of Swords
angst	Page of Cups
apathy	Four of Cups
approachable	Queen of Cups
artistic	Knight of Cups
as above, so below	The Magician
aspiring	Page of Pentacles
attack	Ten of Swords
attainment	Nine of Pentacles
author	Knight of Wands

authority	The Emperor
awakening	Judgement
bad situation	Six of Swords
bad situation	Ten of Swords
balance	Temperance
balanced	Justice
balanced	Two of Pentacles
battle	Five of Wands
battle	Nine of Wands
beautiful things	Queen of Pentacles
beginnings	Death
beginnings	The Fool
beloved	Two of Cups
betrayal	Seven of Swords
betrayal	Ten of Swords
betrayal	Three of Swords
bondage	The Devil
book lover	Page of Swords
bored	Four of Cups
bored	Page of Swords
bottom line	King of Pentacles
break, taking a	Seven of Pentacles
brooding	Four of Cups
business	King of Pentacles
calculating	King of Swords
called to act	Judgement
calmness	Six of Swords
capable	The Magician
carefree	The Sun
cautious	Knight of Pentacles
celebrating	Four of Wands
celebrating	Six of Wands

celebrating	Three of Cups
center of attention	Page of Wands
challenge	Seven of Wands
change	Judgement
change	The Wheel of Fortune
change, sudden	The Tower
charismatic	King of Cups
charismatic	King of Wands
charming	King of Cups
charming	King of Wands
childhood	Six of Cups
choices	The Devil
choices	The Lovers
choosing	Two of Wands
circle of life	The Wheel of Fortune
clear thinking	The Sun
collector	King of Pentacles
comforting	Page of Cups
commitment	Ten of Wands
communicator	Knight of Swords
communicator	Queen of Swords
community	Three of Cups
competence	Three of Pentacles
competition	Five of Wands
completion	The World
compromise	Three of Cups
confidence	Strength
confidence	The Fool
confidence	The Sun
confident	Queen of Wands
conflict	Five of Wands
conflict	Nine of Wands

conflicted	Two of Swords
confrontation	Five of Wands
confrontational	Knight of Swords
confusion	The Moon
connection	Three of Cups
connection	Two of Cups
consciousness	Two of Wands
consequences	Justice
contemplating	Page of Swords
contentment	Nine of Cups
contentment	Ten of Cups
contributions	Three of Pentacles
control	The Emperor
control resources	Nine of Pentacles
controlling	Strength
controlling	The Chariot
controlling	Two of Pentacles
courage	Seven of Wands
courage	Strength
crafts	Page of Pentacles
craftsperson	Three of Pentacles
creation	Ace of Wands
creative	Page of Cups
creative	Queen of Wands
creativity	Ace of Cups
creativity	King of Cups
creativity	The Empress
cunning	Seven of Swords
danger	Eight of Swords
daring	Knight of Wands
deception	Five of Swords
deception	Seven of Swords

deciding	Two of Swords
decision	King of Swords
decision	Seven of Pentacles
decision	Two of Swords
decisive	King of Swords
decisive	The Emperor
dedication	Eight of Pentacles
defeat	Five of Swords
defensiveness	Seven of Wands
deliberate	Page of Pentacles
depression	Four of Cups
depression	Nine of Swords
despair	Five of Pentacles
details	Eight of Pentacles
detached	The Hanged Man
determination	Two of Wands
difficulties	Five of Swords
diligence	Eight of Pentacles
disaster	Ten of Swords
discipline	Nine of Wands
dishonesty	Seven of Swords
dishonor	Five of Swords
dissatisfaction	Eight of Cups
dissatisfaction	Four of Cups
distortion	The Moon
divine wisdom	The High Priestess
documenting	Seven of Pentacles
down to earth	Page of Pentacles
dramatic	Queen of Wands
dreams	Page of Cups
dreams	Seven of Cups
dreams	The Moon

dreamy	Knight of Cups
duality	The Chariot
duality	The Lovers
earth, love of	King of Pentacles
education	The Hierophant
efficient	Knight of Pentacles
efficient	Queen of Swords
effort	Seven of Pentacles
effort	The Chariot
empowered	Judgement
ending	Death
ending	Ten of Swords
ending	Three of Swords
enemy	Eight of Swords
energy	Ace of Wands
energy	Four of Pentacles
energy	Knight of Wands
energy	Page of Wands
energy	The High Priestess
energy	Two of Wands
enlightenment	The Sun
ennui	Four of Cups
enterprise	Ace of Wands
enterprising	King of Cups
enterprising	King of Wands
enthusiasm	Ace of Wands
enthusiasm	Page of Wands
environment	Queen of Pentacles
escaping	Six of Swords
escapism	Seven of Cups
event coordinator	Queen of Pentacles
events	Eight of Wands

evidence	Knight of Swords
excess	Ten of Pentacles
expectation	Three of Wands
expectations	Seven of Pentacles
expecting the worst	Nine of Swords
experience	Ace of Cups
failure	Five of Pentacles
fairness	Justice
family	Queen of Wands
family	Six of Cups
fantasies	Seven of Cups
fate	The Wheel of Fortune
favors	Six of Pentacles
fear	The Devil
fearless	The Fool
feelings	Eight of Cups
feelings, heedless of	Knight of Swords
fertility	The Empress
financial advancement	Ace of Pentacles
financial difficulty	Five of Pentacles
financial security	Knight of Pentacles
flow	Temperance
focused	King of Pentacles
focused	Knight of Swords
foresight	Three of Wands
freedom	The Sun
friend	Page of Cups
friends	Four of Wands
friends	Two of Cups
friendship	Three of Cups
frustration	Five of Cups
full circle	The World

fun	Three of Cups
future	Two of Wands
gatherings	Four of Wands
gender identity	The Lovers
generosity	Six of Pentacles
generosity	The Empress
generous	King of Pentacles
giving	Six of Pentacles
goals	Knight of Swords
goals	Knight of Wands
goals	The Magician
good fortune	Nine of Cups
good health	Nine of Cups
good luck	Ace of Pentacles
good things	Ace of Pentacles
good work	Three of Pentacles
grace	Temperance
grief	Death
grief	Five of Cups
group effort	Four of Wands
guidance	The Hermit
guidance	The Star
guided	Eight of Cups
guilt	Seven of Swords
happiness	Nine of Cups
happiness	Ten of Cups
happy	Four of Wands
happy	Ten of Cups
harmony	Queen of Cups
harmony	Temperance
harmony	Two of Cups
health	Five of Pentacles

impartial	Queen of Swords
impermanence	The Wheel of Fortune
improvement	Eight of Pentacles
impulsive	Knight of Wands
independence	Nine of Pentacles
independence, lost	The Devil
inexperience	The Fool
influences	Eight of Wands
inheritance	Ten of Pentacles
initiations	The High Priestess
innocence	The Fool
innocent	Six of Cups
innovative	Page of Wands
insight	Ace of Swords
insight	The High Priestess
insight	The Tower
inspirational	King of Cups
inspirational	King of Wands
inspirational	Queen of Wands
instinct	The Moon
instinctual	Queen of Cups
instinctual	The Fool
instruction	The Hierophant
integrity, lost	Five of Swords
intelligent	Queen of Swords
interior	Four of Cups
introspection	Four of Cups
introspection	The Hermit
intuition	The High Priestess
intuition	The Star
intuitive	Queen of Wands
invest	Ace of Pentacles

investments	Knight of Pentacles
journey	Six of Swords
joy	The Sun
joy	The Wheel of Fortune
joy	Three of Cups
judged, being	Justice
karma	Justice
known	Eight of Cups
law of attraction	Three of Wands
laws	Justice
lawyer	King of Swords
leader	King of Cups
leader	King of Pentacles
leader	King of Wands
leader	Knight of Wands
leap of faith	The Fool
learning	Page of Pentacles
learning	Three of Swords
letting go	The Hanged Man
limbo	The Hanged Man
lists	Page of Swords
loans	Six of Pentacles
logic	King of Swords
logic	Two of Swords
loneliness	Five of Pentacles
loss	Death
loss	Five of Cups
lost focus	Seven of Cups
love	The Lovers
love	Two of Cups
loyal	Knight of Cups
loyal	Page of Cups

loyal	Page of Pentacles
maintenance	Ten of Wands
manifestation	Three of Pentacles
manipulation	Five of Swords
marginalization	Five of Pentacles
mastering	Eight of Pentacles
maternal	The Empress
measure	Temperance
memories	Six of Cups
mental clarity	Ace of Swords
messages	Eight of Wands
methodical	Knight of Pentacles
mind games	Five of Wands
miserliness	Four of Pentacles
misfortune	Ten of Swords
moderation	Temperance
money	Four of Pentacles
motherhood	The Empress
movement	Eight of Wands
movement	The Chariot
multitasking	Two of Pentacles
mysteries	The High Priestess
nature	The Empress
negative	Five of Cups
new beginning	Ace of Cups
new beginning	Ace of Wands
new dawn	Ten of Swords
new world	Six of Swords
next step	Two of Wands
nightmares	Nine of Swords
nostalgia	Six of Cups
obligations	Ten of Wands

pause	Seven of Pentacles
perfection	The World
performer	Queen of Wands
persisting	Ten of Wands
personality	Knight of Wands
perspective	The Hanged Man
plan	Knight of Swords
pleasure	Nine of Cups
poet	Queen of Cups
policing	Justice
possibilities	The Moon
potential	The Magician
potential	The World
potential	Three of Wands
power	Ace of Swords
powerlessness	Eight of Swords
powerlessness	The Hanged Man
practical	King of Pentacles
practical	Queen of Pentacles
practice	Eight of Pentacles
pride	Eight of Pentacles
pride	Six of Wands
principles	Seven of Wands
prioritizing	Two of Pentacles
progress	Three of Pentacles
project	Ten of Wands
project manager	Queen of Swords
promising	Page of Wands
prosperous	Ten of Pentacles
protection	Six of Swords
protégé	Page of Wands
psychic	Queen of Cups

psychic	The High Priestess
psychic	The Moon
psychologist	Queen of Cups
public speaker	Queen of Wands
quickly	Eight of Wands
reckless	Knight of Wands
readiness	Nine of Wands
realist	Knight of Pentacles
reality	Seven of Cups
reason	Ace of Swords
reasoning	King of Swords
receiving	Six of Pentacles
receptive	Knight of Cups
recognition	Three of Pentacles
reconciliation	Ace of Cups
recognized	Six of Wands
recovery	Four of Swords
reflecting	Seven of Pentacles
regret	Five of Cups
regulations	The Emperor
rejection	Three of Swords
relationship	Ace of Cups
relationship	Ten of Cups
reliable	Knight of Pentacles
religious	The Hierophant
renewal	Judgement
reserves	Four of Swords
resilience	Strength
resourceful	Queen of Pentacles
resources	Page of Pentacles
resources	The Magician
responsibilities	Ten of Wands

sensitive	Page of Cups
sensitive	Queen of Cups
sentimental	Page of Cups
separate	Seven of Swords
serenity	The Star
sexual identity	The Lovers
shining armor	Knight of Swords
simpler times	Six of Cups
solitude	Five of Cups
solitude	The Hermit
something missing	Eight of Cups
sorrow	The Wheel of Fortune
spiritual	Queen of Cups
spiritual awakening	Ace of Cups
spiritual journey	Eight of Cups
spontaneous	Page of Wands
spreadsheets	Page of Swords
stability	Ten of Pentacles
stability	The Emperor
stable	King of Pentacles
stagnant	Four of Pentacles
stagnation	Eight of Cups
stalemate	Two of Swords
stamina	Nine of Wands
still waters	The High Priestess
stories	Page of Cups
strategizing	Seven of Swords
street smart	Page of Swords
strength	Nine of Wands
strengths	Strength
stress	The Tower
stressful efforts	Four of Swords

strife	Five of Wands
strong	King of Wands
stubbornness	Four of Pentacles
student	Page of Swords
stupidity	Seven of Swords
subconscious	The Moon
success	Six of Wands
successful	Ace of Wands
sum of parts	The Magician
sunny	Queen of Wands
support	Three of Cups
supporter	Queen of Wands
sweetness	Six of Cups
systems	The Emperor
systems analyst	Knight of Swords
taking a stand	Seven of Wands
talent	Eight of Pentacles
teacher	Knight of Wands
teacher	The Hierophant
teamwork	Three of Pentacles
tested	Seven of Cups
testing	The Chariot
theft	Seven of Swords
thinking	Ace of Swords
thinking	Page of Swords
thinking	Two of Swords
thoughts, oppressive	Nine of Swords
ties that bind	Three of Cups
tradition	Ten of Pentacles
traditional	King of Pentacles
traditions	The Emperor
tranquility	Queen of Cups

tranquility	Ten of Cups
transformation	Death
transportation	The Chariot
trapped	Eight of Swords
travel	Eight of Wands
travel	Six of Swords
triumph	Strength
troubles	Four of Swords
truth	Ace of Swords
truth	The Tower
truth seeker	Page of Swords
truthful	King of Swords
understanding	Ace of Cups
understanding	The Star
unemotional	Queen of Swords
unethical	Five of Swords
unfair	Five of Swords
union	Two of Cups
unknown	Eight of Cups
unsettled	Two of Pentacles
unstable	Five of Cups
vacation	Four of Swords
validation	Six of Wands
victory	Six of Wands
vigilance	Nine of Wands
visit	Six of Cups
vitality	The Sun
vulnerability	Nine of Swords
waiting	Three of Wands
warm	Knight of Wands
way out, finding a	Eight of Swords
wedding	Four of Wands

welcome	Nine of Cups
wholeness	The World
willful action	The Magician
willpower	Ace of Wands
willpower	King of Cups
willpower	King of Wands
willpower	The Chariot
winning	Ace of Pentacles
winning at any cost	Five of Swords
wisdom	The Hermit
wishes	Seven of Cups
wishes	Nine of Cups
wishes fulfilled	The Star
witty	King of Swords
wonder	Six of Cups
work	Eight of Pentacles
worry	Nine of Swords
yank off bandage	The Tower

Recommended Reading

Nancy Antenucci and Melanie Howard, *Psychic Tarot*

A book for Dreamers and anyone interested in improving their psychic access to the cards. Full of inspiration, guidance, and insight.

Sarah Bartlett, *The Tarot Bible*

A small but dense book of card interpretations with several example spreads. Includes a concise look at correspondences with other esoteric schools of thought.

Joseph Campbell and Richard Roberts, *Tarot Revelations*

Interesting for the foreword by Joseph Campbell and his essay on the Marseilles deck.

Mary K. Greer, *21 Ways to Read a Tarot Card*

An excellent review of many aspects of the tarot with effective exercises.

Mary K. Greer, *Tarot for Yourself*
A classic book that guides you in using the tarot for inner work and self-knowledge.

Mary K. Greer and Tom Little, *Understanding the Tarot Court*
An in depth look at the sixteen court cards, examining them from many angles. Includes exercises, spreads, and comprehensive interpretations.

Anthony Louis, *Tarot Plain and Simple*
An introductory book that has more information on reversals than average.

Barbara Moore, *Modern Guide for Energy Clearing*
A deep look into the energies in our lives. Includes several techniques for building good energetic habits.

Barbara Moore, *Tarot for Beginners*
A good introduction to the tarot that looks at each card from three different decks. Includes samples and exercises for developing your skills.

Sallie Nichols, *Jung and Tarot: An Archetypal Journey*
Long essays about each of the major arcana from a Jungian perspective.

Dan M. Pelletier, *The Process: The Way of the Tarot Reader*
An audiobook that takes a gentle journey to understanding the tarot and bringing its wisdom into your life.

Rachel Pollack, *Seventy-Eight Degrees of Wisdom*
Comprehensive, in-depth card interpretations and explanations of different types of readings.

Rachel Pollack, *Tarot Wisdom*
A wide-ranging book based on many years of tarot experience and research. A classic in the field.

To Write to the Author

If you wish to contact the author or would like more information about this book, please write to the author in care of Llewellyn Worldwide Ltd. and we will forward your request. Both the author and publisher appreciate hearing from you and learning of your enjoyment of this book and how it has helped you. Llewellyn Worldwide Ltd. cannot guarantee that every letter written to the author can be answered, but all will be forwarded. Please write to:

Denise Hesselroth
℅ Llewellyn Worldwide
2143 Wooddale Drive
Woodbury, MN 55125-2989

Please enclose a self-addressed stamped envelope for reply,
or $1.00 to cover costs. If outside the U.S.A., enclose
an international postal reply coupon.

Many of Llewellyn's authors have websites with additional
information and resources. For more information,
please visit our website at http://www.llewellyn.com

GET MORE AT LLEWELLYN.COM

Visit us online to browse hundreds of our books and decks, plus sign up to receive our e-newsletters and exclusive online offers.

- • Free tarot readings • Spell-a-Day • Moon phases
- • Recipes, spells, and tips • Blogs • Encyclopedia
- • Author interviews, articles, and upcoming events

GET SOCIAL WITH LLEWELLYN

Find us on  ✔ @LlewellynBooks

www.Facebook.com/LlewellynBooks

GET BOOKS AT LLEWELLYN

LLEWELLYN ORDERING INFORMATION

Order online: Visit our website at www.llewellyn.com to select your books and place an order on our secure server.

Order by phone:
- • Call toll free within the US at 1-877-NEW-WRLD (1-877-639-9753)
- • We accept VISA, MasterCard, American Express, and Discover.

Order by mail:
Send the full price of your order (MN residents add 6.875% sales tax) in US funds plus postage and handling to: Llewellyn Worldwide, 2143 Wooddale Drive, Woodbury, MN 55125-2989

POSTAGE AND HANDLING

STANDARD (US):(Please allow 12 business days)
$30.00 and under, add $6.00.
$30.01 and over, FREE SHIPPING.

CANADA:
We cannot ship to Canada. Please shop your local bookstore or Amazon Canada.

INTERNATIONAL:
Customers pay the actual shipping cost to the final destination, which includes tracking information.

Visit us online for more shipping options. Prices subject to change.

FREE CATALOG!

To order, call
1-877-
NEW-WRLD
ext. 8236
or visit our
website